A Celtic Model of Ministry

A Celtic Model of Ministry

The Reawakening of Community Spirituality

Jerry C. Doherty

A Michael Glazier Book

THE LITURGICAL PRESS
Collegeville, Minnesota

www.litpress.org

A Michael Glazier Book published by The Liturgical Press.

Cover design by Ann Blattner. Illustration from The Book of Durrow, c. 680 A.D.

1   2   3   4   5   6   7   8

Library of Congress Cataloging-in-Publication Data

Doherty, Jerry C., 1949–
    A Celtic model of ministry : the reawakening of community spirituality / Jerry C. Doherty.
        p.   cm.
    Includes bibliographical references and index.
    ISBN 0-8146-5161-5 (alk. paper)
    1. Church growth.   2. Spirituality—Celtic Church.
    3. Community—Religious aspects—Celtic Church.   I. Title.

BV652.25 .D64   2003
262'.001'7—dc21   2002035252

Contents

Acknowledgments

Numerous people have helped me in the past few years to write and research this book. I would like to thank especially the Rev. Dr. David Keller for his vision, knowledge, and friendship. I owe much to Seabury-Western Theological Seminary and their program in Congregational Development at the Seabury Institute. Special thanks go to the Rev. Dr. Arlin Rothauge for his input and support. St. Deiniol's Residential Library under the direction of its warden, Peter Francis, provided a generous grant in the fall of 2000 to write the manuscript. Thanks go to the Rev. Canon Don Allchin and the Rt. Rev. John Spong for reading the manuscript.

My parish of The Episcopal Church of the Ascension has been most supportive, especially my secretary, Roberta Wilkinson, who has typed countless lines for me.

Most important, I would like to thank my family—my wife, Sheila, and my daughters, Anna and Nia—who never tired of saying, "tell us more about round towers Daddy."

Preface

I believe that to be the people of God today, in the early twenty-first century, beginning a new millennium, we must meditate on the transfiguration of Our Lord, when Jesus went up on the mountain with his disciples (Matthew 17:1-9). It was on the mountain that often the people of God discerned from the Almighty what they must do to follow God.

To go up the mountain, the faithful are looking for a holy place to be with God. We are told of Abraham and his son Isaac. Abraham knew God and he was obedient to his God. He knew that God wanted him to do something. He believed that God wanted him to sacrifice his beloved son, Isaac. It was common among people in those days to sacrifice their firstborn child to the gods. The sacrifice of the first born is what Abraham's God required of him too. So Abraham went up the mountain with his axe ready.

Abraham thought he knew what God wanted. He went up the mountain only to find out that God did not want Isaac, the son he loved. God had other plans in mind. God wanted Abraham and his heart, his devotion.

Moses was leading the people of Israel in the wilderness. He had listened to God. He had acted. The people were free of slavery in Egypt. God had delivered them from bondage at the Passover. God had saved them from the army of Pharaoh at the Red Sea. What now? Moses went up the mountain to meet with God. He was given tablets of stone, the Ten Commandments, the guide for this new community of Israel.

Jesus was told to proclaim the coming of God's kingdom, that God's fulfillment was very near. He taught; he healed; he preached; he fed the people. The people said he was the Messiah, the Anointed One, the one who literally would bring what God wanted into the world. What did God want of him?

He went up the mountain. He was transfigured; he was changed. He and his clothes became dazzling white. Jesus was standing with Moses and Elijah, the two great prophets. Jesus was part of God's plan for the world. He realized what he must do as the Messiah. He must die and rise again.

There are many times in our lives, like these examples, when we need to discern what God would have us do. Like Jesus we seek the presence of God to find the answer. What would God have us do in our time? We need to go up the mountain and find out.

We have to find out what God wants us to do because we live in a time of crisis. Our culture and our country are not doing well. We live in the most violent century of all. We still face the threat of annihilation in a nuclear war. There is a widening gap between the rich and the poor and the poor are increasing in number. There is a "mean spirit" in the world that only seems to grow worse. Once our churches were full; now they are almost empty. The institutions and morals we held dear are no longer true. What should we do? We need to go to the holy place and seek the presence of God, to go up the mountain.

We need to be transfigured. We need to find God and ask what we must do. Perhaps we can be transfigured, changed to bring Christ into the world to become "his Body." If we are made into Christ in the world we can bring back health and salvation to the earth.

As we look for direction in our world maybe we can find the way by retracing our steps. The Church has always been the people of God, Christ in the world. The Church developed in the culture of Rome into what it is today. Is there another cultural context we have lived in to which Christians brought the Gospel? Are there other ways of doing God's work we have done before? Can these ways be a guide and a model for us today? Are those ways a possible blueprint for becoming the hands and feet of Christ in the world, the Body of Christ, his Church, God Incarnate? These questions motivate my research into the relation of Celtic spirituality to our parish life today.

I believe that it is our mission to become the Body of Christ anew in our time. It is our role to bring salvation to the earth. I believe that the parish churches, the faithful gathered together in the local congregations all over the world are the people to accomplish this mission. We are the only people who have the network in place and the understanding to do what needs to be done.

Introduction

A great cultural upheaval is in process around much of the world. The religious beliefs, morals and traditions of the last millennia are being questioned and rejected. We are currently in the most extensive spiritual change since the development of Christianity from Judaism.

The reasons for the upheaval are due to many factors; rapid technological, economic and social change; the sudden unimportance of our ancestral beliefs, customs and values; the break with the land and the past; the rapid movement of money, people and ideas around the world. There is also the pervasive sense of groundlessness and outsidelessness. "Is that all there is? You mean, this is it?"[1]

The vast change has brought a decline in the membership of churches. In the United States most denominations have lost members. When comparing figures recorded by the American Religious Data Archive and the Census Bureau, even those who have increased have not grown much considering the rapid growth in population. The largest percentage growth is the Armenian Apostolic Church of America, which grew by 619 percent between 1980 and 1990. The total membership is only 73,300, made up largely of immigrants from Lebanon. The Roman Catholic Church, the largest church in the United States grew by 5,883,846 persons in the same decade

---

[1] Don Cupitt, *After God: The Future of Religion* (London: Weidenfeld and Nicholson, 1997) 80.

with 53,385,998 total membership. Even with this growth in the Catholic Church there is a second crisis of a shortage of clergy; some clergy serve huge parishes without assistance. Overall, churches grew 12.4 percent during the 1980s with a total increase of 13,753,073. The increases become insignificant in light of the general population growth of the same period; the population of the United States increased 25 million from 1980–1990 with 248 million in 1990. Currently the population of the United States is 287,014,000. The numbers have continued to decline. The Church has lost members in other parts of the world as well. Only one in seven people in the United Kingdom now attend a church regularly. Crisis of ministry and religion continue. If the decline is not abated by the next generation the churches could be virtually empty.

In the midst of this change and decline of religion there have been unprecedented shifts in the world order. The twentieth century was one of tremendous violence. More people died from war and its aftermath in the last century than in all preceding ten thousand years combined. More than half were noncombatants.[2] There have been tremendous changes in ethical behavior. Many people question the future. We are at a critical point in the life of the planet with the threat of environmental disaster. We live in a time of crisis.

My thesis is that the only solution to the problems creating the crises of our time is a spiritual reawakening. People need a relationship with God. They need to form new ways of thinking to deal with new challenges. Only spiritual truth can give us the answers. The people that can bring about this reawakening are the followers of the world religions. In my culture the churches must face the challenge. They are the only resource. The churches have all the tools necessary to be transfigured into the Church God intended us to be.

A further belief is that the early Celtic Christians can help us find a new paradigm, a new way of being the Church in

---

[2] Walter Wink, *The Powers That Be: Theology for a New Millennium* (New York: Doubleday, 1998) 137.

order to meet the challenge. The early Christians in the Celtic lands of Ireland, Wales, Scotland, Cornwall, Brittany, and the Isle of Man, even though they were part of the greater Church, did things differently as a result of their common isolation and culture. Ireland was the only place in the ancient world that the Romans did not touch. It is from the Romans that we inherited most of the Church organization for mission and ministry we have today. This old paradigm is the one currently in use and it is no longer relevant. Perhaps we can learn from people who lived long ago who had a successful way of doing the work of the Church differently than the Roman model. In Wales especially the Romans were part of the society for almost four hundred years. When the legions left in 410 C.E. the Welsh people were left bereft of support, protection and culture. Everything was chaos as much of the world is today. Despite the challenge the Welsh meet the change successfully with their Celtic roots.

A criticism of my thesis is that I cannot use ancient people to prove my assumptions and need for a new model of ministry. Their culture and time were much different than ours. There are similarities, however, the most prominent being the fact that most of the people in their world were not church goers either. We can use what we know of the early Celtic Christians and culture to find new ways of ministry in our time. I am not interested in recreating their church or culture or proving they thought like we do. I believe the Celtic people can provide us with a new model for building the Christian Church now, especially the local congregation.

Recently, other Celtic scholars and students of mission in the church have become interested in the Celtic method of ministry. In 1996 John Finney wrote his book *Recovering the Past: Celtic and Roman Mission*. In the conclusion he writes:

> [W]hen a large group of people are not Christian, living in society which has attitudes and an ethos which is not Christian, then the Celtic model of ministry is more effective. . . . After conversion of a nation or a community when a "Christendom" situation obtains, then a settled Roman pattern is more satisfactory.

> Where there is a "mixed economy"—where Christen-
> dom still has some vestiges of former glory (and such
> communities still exist in many places) we need a mix of
> both Roman and Celtic forms of ministry.[3]

In the year 2000 two books emerged on the subject: *The Celtic Way of Evangelism: How Christianity Can Reach the West . . . Again* by George G. Hunter III, and *Colonies of Heaven: Celtic Models for Today's Church* by Ian Bradley. Both authors believe that the Church can learn from Celtic Christians. In particular Hunter says we can learn five themes from Celtic Christianity:

(1) Work as a team to "identify with the people, engaging in friendship, conversation, ministry and witness."

(2) Focus on monastic community, which prepared people to "live with depth, compassion and power in mission."

(3) A role of imaginative prayer in all settings.

(4) Hospitality in the monastic community inviting all people as guests.

(5) A focus on the experience of those who seek God in the church: you first establish community with people. Within fellowship engage in conversation, ministry, prayer and worship. In time they come to believe and are invited to commit.[4]

Finney agrees with the focus on the seeker. I echo the opinion of both of these writers. In 1998 I completed my doctoral studies in congregational development at the Seabury Institute, part of the graduate programs at Seabury–Western Theological Seminary in Evanston, Illinois. My dissertation,

---

[3] John Finney, *Recovering the Past: Celtic and Roman Mission* (London: Darton, Longman and Todd Ltd., 1996) 141.

[4] George G. Hunter, *The Celtic Way of Evangelism: How Christianity Can Reach The West . . . Again* (Nashville: Abingdon Press, 2000) 47–55.

The Caim Community: Early Celtic Christian Communities as a Model in Parish Ministry, set forth the same types of theories as Finney, Hunter, and Bradley. I have applied the model in ministry for over ten years and have experienced its success. We can develop a new way of thinking about our congregations and a new method of doing ministry in our rural areas, towns, and cities following the Celtic example.

In this book I explore the problems that have caused the decline of the Church and how paradigms we have used are no longer viable. I put forth that we are facing three different crises that are at the same time interconnected. They are a crisis of individualism, a crisis of faith, and a crisis of lifestyle. The crisis of individualism is countered by community. The void created by a crisis of faith is filled by mysticism. The crisis of lifestyle is resolved by direction in leading a Christian way of life.

The way of the early Celtic Christians in fulfilling their Christian mission is a model we can use in meeting the challenges of our time. In the sixth and seventh centuries Irish Christians brought Christianity back to Europe after it was lost with the fall of Rome and the barbarian invasions. Perhaps these ancient Christians are on the road of pilgrimage and evangelism again to yet another people in need of God.

Chapter One
A Crisis of Individualism

The Church has been unable to do the mission of becoming the Body of Christ in the world because it has been affected by and become part of the individualistic culture of today. Because of our culture and our reaction to it serious problems have developed in the Church.

An example is the Episcopal Church, which in 1990, along with the rest of the Anglican Communion, made an incredible declaration. They set aside the 1990s as a "Decade of Evangelism." In the next ten years the Church would concentrate on evangelism, getting new members and bringing people the message of Christ. Yet evangelism has been the work of the Church from its beginning. Why then was it necessary to make such a declaration?

It was necessary because it is a time of crisis; a crisis brought about by a drastic loss of membership in the Episcopal Church as well as other denominations. Between 1966 and 1986 the Episcopal Church lost over a million members so that in 1990 there was only two and a half million baptized Episcopalians in the United States, with the numbers continuing to decline. The crisis is a crisis of evangelism.

Other Christian denominations in the U.S. have had seriously declining membership as well. The Episcopal Church has had a proportional loss similar to the Evangelical Lutheran Church in America, the Presbyterian Church, the United

Methodist Church, and the United Church of Christ. All of these denominations reached their height in membership between 1960 and 1970 and since then have been in steady decline.[1] The Roman Catholic Church is the largest denomination in the United States and is growing but only by a slight increase considering the growth of the population.

In his book *Transforming Congregations for the Future,* Loren Mead points out that the situation is even more drastic than it appears. All of these losses occurred at a time of rapid population growth in the United States. When you compare these denominations as a percentage of the population their decreases are even greater. Their numbers take a "nose dive."[2] People are not receiving the message of Christ in all these denominations and becoming church members. In fact they are responding in the opposite way. The trend continues as we enter the new century.

People seem to be saying the Church is not a relevant part of their lives anymore. The Church is not meeting their personal needs. They are either quitting church altogether, going to other more evangelical churches, or finding new ways to address their spirituality.

There have been many theories given to explain the decline covering a wide spectrum of opinion. These answers often either try to avoid the issue or point to the circumstances causing the problem without giving real solutions. One explanation has been that we count people differently on the local annual reports than we have before. Our figures were inflated and now we have a more realistic picture. Other people have said the decline in church members is due to demographics. The "middle-class" denominations have a lower birthrate than other groups. A further explanation, with some truth, is that many people left the Church because of changes such as the ordination of women, and the revision of the liturgies. With the churches dealing with issues such as the ordination of homosexuals, the

---

[1] Loren B. Mead, *Transforming Congregations for the Future* (New York: The Alban Institute, 1994) 3–5.

[2] Ibid., 8.

possible blessing of same-sex relationships, and inclusive language in liturgy, many people think the Church has become too liberal. It should spend more time "saving souls" and less time involved in controversy.

All of these explanations are not the real answer to what is causing the problem of the Church's drastic decline in numbers. The way we report statistics or demographics is not a real explanation. We have indeed lost members.

Also, the liberal stance of the Church on issues and the changes that have occurred are not a real explanation either. Changes like the revision of services and liturgies and the ordination of women were necessary to carry on the mission of the Church rather than to stifle it.

In my opinion, there is no lack of faith or great disobedience on the part of the people of the Church that is causing the decline. It is my experience that the people are still strong and faithful. In the midst of all the changes in the Church, those who have stayed seem to have increased their faith and commitment. They work harder, give more, and they pray more. Those who left have caused the problem, not those who have stayed.

So what is the problem? What is the cause of our decline? So far these explanations have been inadequate. They tell about only part of the story.

I believe that we are facing a new problem in the Church because our culture is developing in a way unique to the United States and Western Europe. In his book *Habits of the Heart: Individualism and Commitment in American Life,* Robert Bellah describes the development of a certain way of thinking in the United States, a way that was noticed even in the 1830s by Alexis de Tocqueville when he visited America. In his book *Democracy in America,* de Tocqueville describes the mores of our society as "habits of the heart" they are ideas that shape our relationships with others. One of the "habits of the heart" we share as Americans he calls "individualism."

> "'Individualism' is a word recently coined to express a new idea," de Tocqueville wrote. "Our fathers knew only about egoism." Individualism is more moderate and orderly

than egoism, but in the end its results are much the same. "Individualism is a calm and considered feeling which disposes each citizen to isolate himself from the mass of his fellows and to withdraw into his circle of family and friends; with this little society formed to his taste, he gladly leaves the great society to look after itself." As democratic individualism grows, he wrote, "there are more and more people who, though neither rich or powerful enough to have hold over others, have gained or kept enough wealth and enough understanding to look after their own needs. Such folk owe no man anything and hardly expect anything from anybody. They form the habit of thinking of themselves in isolation and imagine that their whole destiny is in their hands." Finally such people come to "forget their ancestors, but also their descendants, as well as isolating themselves from their contemporaries. Each man is forever thrown back on himself alone, and there is danger he may be shut up in the solitude of his own heart."[3]

The American that de Tocqueville describes is present today according to Bellah. Americans are concerned primarily with themselves. For Americans a characteristic problem is justifying the goals of a morally good life. Bellah says, "For most of us, it is easier to think about how to get what we want than to know exactly what we should want."[4]

Americans think that the ultimate values in life are matters of personal choice. One value is success, and success is measured by economic progress. The more money you make, the more successful you must be. People have a great deal of trouble rationalizing their success. However, when their family and marriage suffer because they are working all the time, or when they find they are not happy despite their success, they begin to question their life goals and priorities.

[3] Robert N. Bellah et al., *Habits of the Heart: Individualism and Commitment in American Life* (Berkeley: University of California Press, 1986) 37.
[4] Ibid., 21.

A second value, perhaps the most deeply held in America, is freedom. Freedom concerns both personal and political life. "Yet freedom turns out to mean being left along by others, not having other peoples values, ideas, or styles of life forced upon one, being free of arbitrary authority in work, family and political life."[5] People feel they have personal freedoms that cannot be interfered with by anyone. It is very difficult to form attachments or to cooperate with other people in such a system. Yet at the same time, American life is becoming more integrated and interrelated than ever before.

Americans also hold dear the idea of justice, but to us justice means that all people should have an equal opportunity to pursue what they see as happiness. The great disparity among incomes and living conditions in this society does not matter, we believe, because everyone has the opportunity to get where he or she wants to be.

Bellah says that these values show the ultimate individualism of Americans; we think in personal terms. An example that illustrates this way of thinking is the expression "finding oneself." If you told someone in a remote village in Africa that you had to "find yourself" they would think you were crazy. Yet Americans, because they have to make ultimate decisions and answer the ultimate questions of life, must find themselves. As an American, you must be self-reliant. You must do things on your own without asking for help. You cannot rely on others to make choices for you. You must leave home and develop on your own. If you stay home or live in an extended family, most people view you as weird. You must also leave your parents' church and make your own religious choice. If you do happen to choose the same church as your parents, it must be a conscious decision. As a result, millions of Americans are on a constant spiritual search, "church-shopping," yet never quite finding what they are looking for.[6]

[5] Ibid., 23.
[6] Ibid., 55.

Americans also believe in work. If you do not work you are not worth much. It doesn't matter what you do as long as you work. If you work hard enough, you will be rewarded.[7]

Americans believe in pursuing a "lifestyle." Each person must choose how he or she will live. Each must find the ultimate meaning of life; there must be a "ground" or key which they make all decisions. Bellah even interviewed Americans who replaced the word "soul" with the word "self" as they spoke![8] Americans must make all decisions individually, even about the ultimate meaning of life.

This is the culture to which the Church is trying to minister in our country. Recent national statistics reflect this picture. In a 1990 Gallup Poll, most Americans said they believed in a personal God and in Jesus Christ as the Son of God. Eight out of ten Americans consider themselves Christians. Yet only four out of ten people knew who delivered the Sermon on the Mount! Only a slightly higher percentage could name the four Gospels. The poll showed a big gap between "believers" and "belongers." Most Americans feel you don't have to go to church to be religious or believe in God. Nor is the level of personal and social responsibility much different between believers and nonbelievers.[9] Americans feel that religion is a private matter, separate from their daily lives. Because religion is so private, it does not enter into the world.

Not only must Americans ultimately choose their religion; many people develop their own. One person Bellah interviewed had even named her "faith" after herself, calling it "Sheilaism." Sheila described her faith in this way: "I believe in God. I'm not a religious fanatic. I can't remember the last time I went to church. My faith has carried me a long way. It's Sheilaism. Just my own little voice." As Bellah comments, "this suggests the logical possibility of over 220 million American religions, one for each of us."[10] This individual

[7] Ibid., 65–66.

[8] Ibid.

[9] Marianne Borg and Doley Patterson, "American Faith in the 1980's: An Interview with George Gallup," *Crossings*, XVI, 1.

[10] Bellah et al., *Habits of the Heart*, 221.

way of thinking has made religion in the United States very pluralistic. There are thousands of different religious groups in America. The potential, as Bellah points out, if for every person to be his or her own religion.

In the beginning we did not think this way; it developed over time. The Puritan John Winthrop gave his famous "city on a hill" speech in Salem harbor in 1630, just before landing to begin building in America. He said, "We must delight in each other, make others' conditions our own, rejoice together, mourn together, labor and suffer together, always having before our eyes our community as members of the same body."[11]

Winthrop had a beautiful vision of community in the New World. Many of the founding fathers had other opinions, however. Being Deists, they believed religion could be found by reason alone. Thomas Jefferson said, "I am a sect myself." Thomas Paine said, "My mind is my church."[12] The principle of the separation of Church and state was to protect people from any religion forcing itself on them; they were free to develop their own religious ideas.

Individualism is not all bad; it has helped the United States to develop as a country and to lead for a time the industrial nations of the world. It has protected us from putting our trust in one leader or having all the answers to the questions of life. Unfortunately, it has also closed us to relating with others as members of a community. As de Tocqueville predicted, we are "shut up in the solitude of our own hearts."[13]

Community is what the word "church" really means. The word used by early Christians such as Paul that we translate, as "church" is the word *ekklesia*. Roughly it means "the gathering of those who believe in Christ, in community"[14] or those who are "called out." Another word that is often translated as "church" is the word "koinonia" or "fellowship." Most

[11] Ibid., 28.
[12] Ibid., 223.
[13] Ibid., 37.
[14] Wayne A. Meeks, *The First Urban Christians: The Social World of the Apostle Paul* (New Haven and London: Yale University Press, 1983) 108.

Christians believe in the ultimate community of believers in Christ across space and time. Even if we don't believe it, we base our religion around it. We believe in the Church as community. Is it any wonder we have trouble relating to a culture that is becoming more and more individualistic? No wonder we cannot agree about what the Church believes or what we are doing as a Church body. No wonder we are pointing fingers at each other, blaming someone else for the demise of the Church. In such a society, there can be little doubt why a group of people leaves the Church each time it makes a corporate decision or abides by a past one.

The problem arises from being a church community in an individualistic culture. Everything our society stands for tends to lead people away from the Church rather than toward it. The way of our culture is not the way of biblical faith; it is not the way of the Church, the Body of Christ. The sooner we understand this distinction the sooner we will be able to take the message of Christ to America and to the Western world.

Chapter Two

The Solution: Community

In a society where the Church is trying to respond to individualism we need more community. The Church so far has often responded by using short-term events to form temporary communities hoping that the shared feelings will stick when people get home. Camps, retreats, weekend events are examples of programs that can draw people into a community feeling in just a few days. Problems surface after these events when the participants get home to their local parish and find no real community activity there and get depressed and discouraged. They may become an exclusive group to the extent that they break away entirely from the whole body and begin meeting on their own. It takes only a few experiences of people expecting instant community in programs for us to realize that the only lasting community is long-term community in daily living.

The major concern in most denominations is to keep the community of the church alive, as American culture becomes more individualistic. Unfortunately, the movements of the past four decades, both within and without the Church, had not always served well to promote community. People have left the Church, citing these changes as their reason. Although these changes were necessary to do the mission of the Church and to establish true community, this necessity has not been obvious to most American individualists. They have often concluded instead that the Church was not meeting their personal needs, and that they could just as well find God on their own.

Yet we know that people hunger for a community experience often without realizing it. They shop for churches, searching for one that will fill their spiritual needs in some undefined way. They look for a feeling they often describe only as "warm." When they don't find it they move on—to another church, to another religion, maybe even to a private faith of their own. Those people who remain in the Church request more fellowship events, coffee hours, potlucks, even when the church calendar is full of fellowship events, coffee hours, and pot lucks already. "I never get to share my faith with others" is an often-repeated complaint that shows a need for intimacy and spiritual kinship. People come to church irregularly hoping to fulfill their spiritual lives, but go away disappointed. The church, meanwhile, rushes to develop new programs, better advertisements, and more evangelizing techniques expecting to attract people and keep them in the church. Sometimes the strategies work and people come to stay. However, the result may be a still larger congregation of individualists, which is led by clergy who are taking on the impossible task of meeting every single person's unique, personal need.

Who can best fulfill the American desire for community? At first glance some churches seem to be highly successful at this challenge. But often these congregations are not true communities. No one is welcome who disagrees or behaves differently from their accepted standards; they are exclusive sects, not true communities.

Although we have community it is hard to define. M. Scott Peck says it is like electricity. You can explain how a lamp works, for example, until you plug it into the wall socket and it connects with the power source. Then "there are certain questions about electricity, despite its known physical laws, that even the most advanced electrical engineer cannot answer. That is because electricity is something larger than we are."[1]

---

[1] M. Scott Peck, *The Different Drum: Community Making and Peace* (Simon and Schuster: New York, 1987) 59.

Like electricity, community is larger than we are, precious, impossible to grasp. But also, like electricity, community exhibits certain characteristics that show when and where it exists. In his book *The Different Drum: Community Making and Peace,* M. Scott Peck lists the signs of community. They are inclusivity, realism, contemplation, healing and conversion, and spirit.[2] Any group of people can be a community if they have these attributes. If a church is a real community these characteristics exist.

First, community is *inclusive.* Members must be committed to include everyone, to resolve differences, to reach solutions for disagreements that everyone can live with. To be a church, a community, we must include everyone. It is often easier to exclude people unintentionally than to work on intentionally including everyone.

Churches are very good at excluding other people. Our traditions make it difficult to change anything. We still use words and music in our services that most people do not understand or enjoy. We still do most things like we did them in the 1950s. We use the same format, the same bulletin, the same music, and the same words as before. We do this because it is "in good taste." When in fact it excludes people who are not like us. It attracts our particular ethnic groups traditionalists, but not the general public.

We also think everyone understands what we say. In most bulletins today in liturgical churches we still include the *sursum corda,* the *Gloria in excelsis,* and the "doxology" without ever telling someone where they are in the liturgy or what they mean. We think people should know. Obviously, if we are going to include everyone we have to bend a little or much depending on the circumstance.

We are excluding people, however, because more and more people in our society have never been to church, let alone understand Latin or Church tradition from the Middle Ages![3]

---

[2] Ibid., 63–76.

[3] George G. Hunter, *Church for the Un-Churched* (Abingdon Press: Nashville, 1996) 20.

I am not saying we should abandon our tradition or change everything. Some people like what we do very much but we are reaching new people who are like us, not people outside of the Church.

By assuming people know about our faith and who we are, we immediately exclude them. There is a common belief that "church people" know the answers to life's problems. If you don't know what "church people" know you are not quite as good. The very word "evangelism" in many people's minds represents exclusion. The emphasis is on exclusive beliefs and special knowledge. Some people believe that the purpose of evangelism is to convert people from one set of beliefs, which are wrong or misguided, to a belief in Jesus. Over two-thirds of those who have left the Church do not believe that the Church should convert people to one right way of believing. They do not agree "that the absolute truth for humankind is in Jesus Christ."[4] They believe that Jesus Christ may hold many answers, but we should not exclude other religions or cultures from having the presence of God in them. In including others it might be better to tell people that our faith has an important value for us rather than an exclusive revelation of God.[5] We can include everyone better by simply showing them we live life different than society. We live in compassion and show it in our behavior.[6] We need to tell people that faith is not having all the answers. Our faith lives with the ambiguities and problems of life through the support of God in Christ. Faith is a search for relationships and the presence of God in our often-troubled lives. As Celtic Christians put it, "you can't go on a journey to find God unless you take God along."[7]

[4] James R. Adam, *So You Can't Stand Evangelism?: A Thinking Person's Guide to Church Growth* (Cowley Publications: Cambridge and Boston, 1997) 12.

[5] Ibid., 22.

[6] Ibid., 34.

[7] Ester de Waal, *The Celtic Way of Prayer: The Recovery of the Religious Imagination* (Hodder and Stoughton: London, Sydney, Auchland, 1996) 10.

Do we have programs to help people on a faith journey with all of its trials? Congregations can spend a great amount of time and energy taking care of the people that are already there. Are we assuming everyone believes the same definition of faith as those in church? Or, do we have programs that help people who are not part of the congregation on their faith journey?

Do we even have ministry to those not in power in our church? Do we serve youth, young adults, people of color, or women? To be an inclusive community we must intentionally try to include everyone, especially those not in our midst. When people join together in a parish community differences of opinion will arise and people are committed to stay around to resolve them, not threatening to quit the group if they don't get their way. When we quit the parish because we don't agree with everyone we only exclude ourselves. People say, "I don't go to church to fight. It should be a place where everything is peaceful." The truth is that where people gather there will always be conflicts. However, in a mature community conflicts are resolved.

A healthy community resolves conflicts by reaching consensus. Consensus does not mean that everyone is converted to the same way of thinking. It means that people chose to agree. It means that everyone gives a little in order to follow the decision of the community.

Secondly, a community is *realistic*. This requirement will come as a surprise to most people outside the Church who see it in an opposite way as sublimely unrealistic. They doubt that the lofty goals expressed in the Church's vision of the reign of God can ever be achieved. Peace on earth, sinlessness, a world without hunger are all impossible dreams. What makes a community realistic is not the practicality of its goals but the fact that everyone feels free to speak openly and honestly. An honest, open church community knows it is not perfect and knows it will accomplish only a few of the ultimate goals of Christianity. If people can speak honestly the likelihood is that realistic decisions can be reached about the best small steps to take toward those ultimate goals.

Many Americans believe that churches are out to brainwash them, to make them into "religious fanatics," or even worse like "church people."[8] They fear being controlled by a charismatic preacher, becoming a member of a cult. Cults do exist, certainly, but there is a foolproof way to tell one from a true church community. If the group agrees on every issue, if a powerful leader controls all others without respecting their opinions, if the church exudes unrelieved "sweetness and light," then it probably is a cult or a very exclusive group. Groups can do great evil where free discussion is suppressed. On the other hand, if everyone speaks his or her mind, if everyone's opinion is heard and valued, if conflicts and arguments occur and are resolved, then it is a realistic community.

Thirdly, a community is *contemplative* meaning; it examines itself. When it is unhealthy in any aspect, it recognizes the problem and takes steps to heal itself. Lack of health will certainly occur. The notion that the Church is for perfect people is a myth that we tend to perpetuate by taking pride on dressing right, praying right, behaving right, and being right when we go to church. The implication is that everyone who isn't perfect should stay home. The truth is that we are all imperfect, broken people. We are in a church precisely because we are not perfect, are not in control, and do not have all the answers.

An example of a true community, other than a church community, is Alcoholics Anonymous. Members of AA know they are hurting, know they are desperate, know that if they don't quit drinking they will die. The first words out of an AA member's lips are an admission of brokenness: "I'm an alcoholic." That one true admission creates community. When imperfection is admitted honestly, healing occurs. Members of AA never miss their meeting, no matter where they are. They will go out of their way to help a fellow member in need, whether friend or stranger. Their meetings are contagious. They are in community.

How many church people admit who they are without reservation? How many Christians share their faith and their stories openly within their parish church? We seldom allow ourselves to know the healing power of admitting brokenness.

---

[8] Hunter, *Church for the Un-Churched*, 59.

The fourth characteristic of community is the capacity for *healing and converting.* True community is a safe place to admit and express hurts, joys, and doubts. It is a place to begin life over again. How many of us see our church as a safe place? Can we admit our problems, sins, bad feelings to others there, and begin again? In my opinion most of us would probably say "no." It's too scary to tell others our problems and sins because then they would know how weak and imperfect we really are. For us, confession is a private thing, not public. The Church must be a place where we can honestly admit our brokenness and begin a new life, over and over again.

Finally, a true community has a *spirit,* the spirit of peace and love. Spirit is the quality many people are looking for when they visit any group or organization they would consider joining. Especially, they seek this spirit in the church community. They would identify the spirit as the "warm feeling" or a feeling of contentment or fulfillment from being with the community for a period of time. It is the energy that is present when people feel a spirit in their community. Often people can give their community an identity, what the spirit feels like in their midst. In the Church we call the spirit the Holy Spirit, the very Spirit of God, a person of the Holy Trinity. It is the feeling and presence of spirit that is one of the main signs of true community. It really is the goal of community, especially parish church community, to have the spirit present. It is what makes a parish community, the church or the *ekklesia.*

The Church desperately needs to become the community it is meant to be. The formation of community in our congregations should be our main task. It is the only way, in my opinion, we can change our fragmented culture. The Church is not doing well in our country or in other Western nations because it was formed to be a community. At the same time this truth is our greatest asset, because God is most present in community. It is God that people need in their lives. It is an absence of spirituality, the feeling of the presence of God, which has brought our society to the brink of destruction. If we can become God's true community, the Church, we can change the world. This is a great challenge I believe only the churches can meet.

What all Christian denominations need to recover is an understanding that we are the people called by God in community. We need to understand that in the whole body of the Church Christ is truly present. Until we restore the theology of community to the Church we will continue to be ineffectual in taking the message of Christ to our world.

We must admit that the vast majority of our church congregations are not really communities at all but are doing a more or less good job of faking it. This is no one's fault, really; most of us have never experienced enough community to recognize it. We just know we are looking for something we cannot find. Community is not easy. It requires a lot of hard work. Yet difficult as it is to achieve and maintain, community is worth all the effort because it is what we are called to by God. Once we have attained it we will not want—indeed, we will not be able—to settle for anything less.

Because we have never experienced community we often have wrong ideas and images of what it must be like. The most usual image is that a church is a place where people's personal needs are met—a place where no one is unhappy or dissatisfied. Who meets these needs? Perhaps the church board, the powerful people of the parish, but more likely it is the priest or minister. He or she must please everyone, know what everyone needs or wants, and fill each person's expectations. He or she must be in control. If this doesn't happen, as realistically it cannot happen, the clergy are not doing a good job.

The notion that a person or group of people must control everyone else is not community but what is commonly referred to as "codependency." It is a dysfunctional, addictive aggregation of people afraid to say what they are thinking or reveal their emotions. Unhappily, it is the way many of our churches function.

A dysfunctional group lacks realism. People are not open or trusting enough honestly to speak their minds and hearts. The clergy are seen to be especially holy, always in possession of the answers. A parishioner who does admit problems and risks going to clergy with them may leave the community in shame because now the minister knows them too well. Where people are free to admit their common brokenness and vulnerability, their sinfulness, their need of redemption, community has a chance to form. In such a place, clergy are seen to have an important ministry of service and leadership by virtue of their training, experience, and commitment, but to possess no lock on virtue, no pipeline to heaven. As in the biblical idea of community, people gather in their common need of God and of healing.[9] This is the first phase of community formation.

While speaking honestly is an important initial step to community, it is not easy because once honesty happens, differences start to come out. There are open disagreements, which lead to the second phase of community building, the phase of chaos.[10] Everything seems out of control. In panic, some people try returning to agreement and a false sense of harmony by dishonesty. Becoming angry, others blame each other, blame the church board and the clergy, claiming that if only the leaders had been in control, this would never have happened. Emotional arguments and verbal attacks result. Some leave, saying that church should be a place of peace and contentment not bitter dissension. They look for, and too often find, a church that is a pseudo-community although it makes them feel better. The time of chaos is truly a desert time and there are always those who, like the people of Israel, want to go back to the security of slavery in Egypt. Freedom seems too much to bear. It is scary.

Once a group gets through the turmoil of chaos, the next phase is emptiness. All seems lost. People ask, "Where do we go from here?" They are afraid; they can't see what lies ahead. It may even seem that God has abandoned God's people. Now the church will either go back to faking community or will bravely move ahead into the unknown.

If it does not go back, the result is true community. The signs will be obvious and manifest. The church will be inclusive, demonstrating a commitment to reaching consensus

---

[9] Paul D. Hanson, *The People Called: The Growth of Community in the Bible* (Harper and Row: San Francisco, 1986) 3.

[10] Peck, *The Different Drum,* 90.

rather than expecting an individual or a group to control decision-making. It will be honestly realistic. It will be contemplative, able to consider its faults and committed to change when change is needed. It will be a place where everyone feels safe, free to admit imperfection and brokenness, a place where healing and conversion are not only possible but usual. It will be a place where the faith and the Holy Spirit of love are kept alive.

All this is a great deal of work. Freedom is never easy. Yet once a church reaches community it must be maintained at all costs. For it is in community that God in Christ resides.

The early Church leaders acted to maintain community despite challenges from within and without the Church. The Montanists, a second-century C.E. apocalyptic movement, expected that there would be a speedy outpouring of the Holy Spirit on the Church and saw the first manifestations of the outpouring on their leaders. The presence of the Holy Spirit and ascetical practices would prepare them for the Second Coming of Christ. They resented those Christians who did not follow their practices and were lax, in their opinion, in their lifestyle. They forbade second marriages, condemned lenient fasts, and would not accept back those who fled persecutions.[11] Their actions began to divide the Church.

Another heresy that threatened to divide the early Church was Arianism. The Arians said that Christ was a type of demi-God who is neither God nor man. They tried in this way to explain the impossibility, in their thinking, that Christ could be a human being and God as well.[12] Docetism was another. Docetists claimed that Jesus was not human at all, but only appeared that way.

Gnosticism was a further heresy. The Gnostics were a diverse group who taught that salvation could be attained by special spiritual knowledge. To have this *gnosis* or enlighten-

[11] Elizabeth A. Livingstone, ed., *The Concise Oxford Dictionary of the Christian Church* (Oxford: Oxford University Press, 1977) 344.

[12] Linwood Urban, *A Short History of Christian Thought* (Oxford: Oxford University Press) 62–63.

ment a person had to be one of them.[13] Others could not achieve salvation. These heresies and others were all dealt with in the councils of the Church such as Nicaea in 325 C.E. and Chalcedon in 451 C.E. The church authorities said all of these heresies could not be part of the Church. All of these disagreements caused the church to become fragmented and divided church communities.

How do we restore community to the Church? The first priority is to accept wholeheartedly that this is what the Church is meant to be. We are God's community, no more and no less. We must believe that the only way to be God's people and experience to the fullest the joy of knowing God is to be as one. We must do everything possible to be honest with each other, to break our old pattern of "faking it," of pretending that everything is fine in our lives. Priests and ministers must openly acknowledge that they cannot fulfill the all-too-common expectation of being in control, of being able to fix things for everyone. Only by freely admitting un-health can the Church become healthy again. We must agree that we are the oppressed, desperately in need of God. It is then that God will save us. As the people of Israel cried out to God in slavery in Egypt, we too must cry out for deliverance.

Second, we must admit our need of God by taking our ministry work as Christians seriously. Not only must we state our faith, we must think about what we will do and how our lives will change because of what we believe. We must see, and enable others to see, that when we are part of God's community we become part of Christ. Christ is present in us. By the grace of the Holy Spirit we are the Body of Christ working to change the world, to bring about daily the "shalom" of God. When people realize this ultimate purpose their baptism becomes meaningful and exciting.

Third, we must restore the teaching ministry of the early Church, adapting it to our time. We cannot make instant Christians. The Christian life is a pilgrimage of growth in Christ. Once a person admits his or her need of God and asks

---

[13] Ibid., 75–78.

for baptism or wishes to be part of the church community we are obligated to provide the best instruction possible. It is an education in the faith and the way to a spiritual life in Christ. Until people see themselves as part of the biblical community of God, they will not fully understand the liturgy or services and will only be going through the motions. The sacraments are symbols in action. People cannot recognize the action if they do not fully understand the symbols.

When children too young to be taught the faith are baptized, we must strive to have their parents and sponsors in teaching programs. How can they rear their children in the faith when they themselves do not know of it and do not live it? Others who are confirmed church members should be encouraged to join classes too, so that they can renew their baptismal vows with greater understanding of what they mean.

All of us would benefit from this kind of renewal. As the Church we must admit together our brokenness and our need of God. We must take the life, death, and resurrection of Christ as our own and share in the life that it brings us. We must truly declare our faith in baptism and become the Body of Christ in the world.

Fourth, we must know the story of the community to which we belong; we must know the Bible. Current studies and polls reveal that, by and large, we do not know it. We must understand the ways in which God's community in the world began with Abraham, how God's people were saved from oppression in Egypt. We must realize fully how God goes to those in need, how God searches for us and we for God. We must comprehend how we have been delivered from our own oppression of disobedience to God by our Lord Jesus Christ. We must know the Bible to be the story of the people called.

Finally, the life of the community of God, in the liturgical churches is based on the great symbolic action of our oneness in Christ gathered together, receiving the bread and wine, the thanksgiving for our deliverance, the Eucharist or Lord's Supper. As the Jews observed the Passover, the memory of their deliverance from bondage and the gathering of the community of Israel, Christians gather together to remember their deliverance from sin and oppression and God in Christ is present in our midst. When they remember and share a brief moment in time the "shalom" of God has come and the kingdom is here in our own time and space. People who minutes ago were at each other's throats come together in peace as Christ in our midst restores community. Being renewed they go out to bring the message of salvation in Christ to the world.

There is a problem in our thinking in terms of community enough to recognize that Christ is present among us in the Holy Eucharist. We think of God as existing somewhere out of the world. We do not really believe in the Incarnation the fact that God is a human being born as Jesus Christ, God in the flesh as we are. Consequently, we don't really believe in the Resurrection as Christ risen and present with us here today. As the Platonic philosophy separated the flesh from the Spirit, so we tend to think of spiritual reality as not of this world and as personal rather than communal. In our individualistic society, we tend to think of the Holy Spirit as a personal possession given to those of us chosen by God. We must understand that the Holy Spirit is the possession of the community of the Church and given to all the people, not to individuals. If God had intended his message for a special few he would have gone only to them. You and I would never have known about Jesus Christ. Only when we see ourselves as the community of God will we be able to know with all of our being that we are the Easter people experiencing Christ in our midst.

Once we have reached true community in our churches we will find ourselves less confined. Freed from our own pretenses, we will be enabled to reach out to others who are in need of us. Reaching out we will feel Christ's presence most strongly because God is with us in the world whenever we help each other. We will know then that the kingdom is with us, that God's shalom is inevitable and in fact is here, now.

Our country, indeed the world, is in a spiritual crisis. Our individualism is killing us. Working together can only solve the greatest problems we have, the threat of nuclear war, world hunger and poverty, the environmental crisis. Eventually, if we are to survive, all people of the world must see themselves as a community in which their brothers' and sisters' welfare is their own. Ultimately we must see ourselves as part of the community of all creation.

I believe the Church is uniquely situated to put the idea of God's community before the world by demonstration in local parishes. We have a fine example in the early Church and Celtic Christianity. We have the tools in our Scripture, our liturgy, and our tradition. The people of the Church are God's people called to relationship with God. Let us answer the call and once more become God's true community, the Church of our Lord Jesus Christ! Once we answer the call of God in community Christ will be present in our midst. The fulfillment of God will come by the work of God's people. If we are truly the Church we will succeed because "who can be against us if God is with us?"

We have talked about the need to be changed and transfigured in our time so that we may better do the work of Christ in the world. The world and the Church are in crisis. The crisis is mainly brought about by our individualistic culture. People have an inability to think about anyone but themselves. God, however, is most present in community. We can see that one of the main themes in the story of God's people, the Bible, is community. God has established God's presence in the world in Our Lord Jesus Christ, in relationship with us individually as well as with others in community. It is the lack of this community that has caused a void of spirituality in our time. Our culture needs community. It is the challenge of the Church to become the community it is meant to be. The Church is the only group that can do this task in our world. We need to become God's community established with the Eucharist, the teaching of the apostles, the Bible, and action and outreach as our basis. How can we do this in our time? Can we reclaim the ways of the early Church? Are these guides for us to become God's community, the Church?

There have been basically two ways or paradigms that the Church has been organized to do mission and ministry in the past. The first one of these ways of thinking is what has been called the "Apostolic Paradigm." The apostolic way of doing things was successful in its time. It brought about God's community in an antagonistic, pluralistic, anxiety-ridden culture of Rome.

The second paradigm, which is fading rapidly in our time, is the "Christendom Paradigm" that developed after the Edict of Milan, which made Christianity the official faith of the Roman Empire.

The Church in response to the culture of the time developed both of these paradigms. What is needed now is a new paradigm, a way of thinking in the Church that can respond successfully to our culture. I believe it must be a paradigm that will bring about true community in the Church. This is the most important response we can make to our culture. Out of God's community, the Church, real evangelism of our culture can occur.

The Apostolic Paradigm developed in response to the culture outside of the early Church. "How was God calling them to relate to the wider world?" the Church asked. The central reality of the early Church was the community, those "called out," the *ekklesia*. They were called out of the world and the surrounding world culture was basically hostile to them. They developed a way of thinking in response to this culture. They could not be true to the teachings of Jesus if they did not confront the antagonistic Greco-Roman culture around them. The mission frontier was at their very door. They called the confrontation with the world "witnessing," the Greek word for which is "martyr." Indeed, many of them did die speaking to the hostile outside environment.[14]

Because the community was so important in this hostile world the form of entry into the Church, baptism, was all-important. There were elaborate programs of training, study, and ritual for candidates in baptism. Those initiated into the community had to know the principles of the faith and sacraments, the story of the community, and especially show a change of behavior from those in the outside culture, the "pagans," they called them, the name for those outside the city. Especially, the person joining the Church must know what

---

[14] Loren B. Mead, *The Once and Future Church: Reinventing the Congregation for a New Mission Frontier* (New York: The Alban Institute, 1991) 10–12.

they were getting into. Belonging to the community could cost you your life.

The second paradigm is known as the Christendom Paradigm. It is ironic that it came as a result of the "success" of the apostolic Church. It began when Emperor Constantine was converted to Christianity and named it the official religion of the Roman Empire in 313 C.E. This changed the orientation of Church thinking inside out. Now the world surrounding the Church, the world formerly hostile to the Church, was the Church. Law now identified the Church with the Empire. No longer was a Christian on the frontier of mission: they did not need to witness as before, in fact they lived their Christian faith by being a responsible citizen of the new Christian culture.[15] It became the soldier's job to be the evangelist because when new lands were conquered they became Christian too. Christianity and the borders of the Empire were the same: everyone living inside the borders was of the faith.

There were several important dimensions to this change. Loren Mead, in his book *The Once and Future Church,* points these out and how much they still affect our thinking today:[16]

1. There was a unity of the sacred and secular. The bishops now worked for the government. They worked together with princes and kings on things "theological"; for example Constantine took a big role in the Council of Nicaea in 325 C.E.

    This leftover way of thinking is still present in our thinking today. Even though Church and state are separate in the United States, our political leaders still have semi-religious status. We still expect a certain Christian morality from them. There is a semi-worship of the flag and patriotism. Religion often is political such as the emergence of the "Moral Majority" in the 1970s and 1980s. America has a certain "civil religion."

---

[15] Ibid., 14.
[16] Ibid., 13–22.

2. Mission became far off rather than at the front door. Mission became the task of foreign policy. Mission was to convert those pagans outside the boundaries. It also was to protect those Christians inside the boundaries of the Empire, especially in the late Roman Empire. "Conversion" was often by the sword. This lead to the Crusades, and "just" wars. Gradually it led to missionaries being sent to "pagan lands" in the nineteenth century. Their task was to convert the "uncivilized" to Christianity but also to the dominant culture of Christendom. This thinking is still prevalent. Mission is in foreign lands. America is a "Christian nation."

3. Congregations became parishes. With the new paradigm, the local church communities stopped being a tight group surrounded by a hostile world. The "hostile world" became the parish. The church, simply to divide the area administratively, established parish boundaries. This was all organized by an efficient Roman hierarchical system. Bishops were in charge of dioceses, which were in turn divided into parishes administered by priests, and deacons had the job of taking care of those in need until their job was supplanted later on.

   This thinking still prevails. Clergy think of their parish as "turf." We often think people are converted just because they are from the neighborhood. Ministry is controlled and done by the clergy alone. Deacons still struggle to take their rightful place in the ministry of the Church. Lay ministry is still a radical issue in many areas of the Church.

4. There was a drive for unity. The only way to govern the vast Empire was to establish complete unity. Heretics were driven out. The Church decided what was right and wrong in belief. Anyone outside the belief system was asked to conform or be an "outlaw." This led to the torture and death of those who did not conform. The Reformation was really born out of

the formation of many nations within the former boundaries of the Empire. The Renaissance also championed the thinking of the individual in new ways.

The remains of this old paradigm are still prevalent. Religious groups seldom think anything goes on outside of their particular denomination. Denominations are in strong competition for converts. Some churches actually claim to be the only "true" Church in Christianity.

5. The religious role of the laity became to "be a good citizen" and never question the government or hierarchy. How many of us still feel guilty when we question authority and let the ministry fall exclusively on those ordained to it?

6. The calling of the layperson was to be a good citizen but also to support those "in mission" far off. They sent supplies to those in the mission field. The missionaries purpose was to take the "one way" of Christianity established in the unity of the Empire to those outside it's boundaries. Unfortunately, as it has been pointed out we still think of mission as far off and that our job is only to send CARE packages on an occasional basis. Missionaries still have the reputation of evangelists as teaching the only "one true way" of belief.[17]

It is Loren Mead's belief that presently we are between paradigms. A new paradigm is arriving as the old one is no longer working and it makes us profoundly uncomfortable. "We no longer can assume everyone is a Christian. We can no longer can assume that the wider community is a unit of the religious world living out values derived from the Gospel."[18] We are returning to features of the apostolic age because there are some similarities in our culture to the apostolic era. The coming into the community, baptism, has become key. In-

[17] Ibid., 25.
[18] Ibid., 26.

deed, certain elements of the early Church, the catechumen-
ate, and the Easter Vigil and the baptismal covenant, have
emerged to help us live the covenant of baptism. All of these
changes in between paradigms make us uncomfortable because we still cling to the old ones. We Christians stick with
tradition. These changes do not comply with the Christendom paradigm so we resist them. At the same time, they do
not adequately respond to our culture today.

Our culture is more diverse than ever before in Christendom.[19] We have to relate to diverse cultural groups. The
boundary between religious and secular is ambiguous. We
argue over where and when to teach religion. We also have all
of our individual beliefs and values in our individualistic culture to contend with. People are not always hostile to the
church. In fact they are more or less indifferent, they simply
don't think the church makes a difference in their lives or the
world. In a survey of people who had dropped out of the Presbyterian Church it was shown that

> Many are not angry or disillusioned, they simply find
> life outside the church attractive and relatively fulfilling.
> For them the *need* for church is not convincing, nor are
> there as many forces in society encouraging or support-
> ing church membership.[20]

The role of clergy is also changing. Authority is questioned
and some clergy fight for control of the situation. They want
to perpetuate the old days of clericalism when clergy were
respected and "in charge." Likewise, the role of bishops and
other judicatories and Church administrators is changing.
They struggle to administer a unit of the old Christendom
paradigm. They have increasing demands on them and their
diocese or districts amid shrinking resources.

I agree that we are living in a time between paradigms. The
old ones, especially the Christendom way of thinking, do not

---

[19] Loren B. Mead, *More Than Numbers: The Ways Churches Grow*
(New York: The Alban Institute, 1993) 37.
[20] Mead, *The Once and Future Church,* 24.

work well. At the same time the new ways that are emerging are not always what is needed. Especially in our individualistic culture, as it has been shown, we are facing something new that has reached crisis proportions. We are losing true community. There is a paradigm that could give us a new beginning and become a guide. This guide is rooted in our Christian past.

Chapter Three

Celtic Spirituality and Community

My thesis is that a new model for thinking and building ministry today especially in the local congregation is founded in the example of the early Christian communities in Ireland, Wales, Brittany, Cornwall and Scotland and the Isle of Man. One problem with our world is that we have developed into an individualist society that has become fragmented and uncaring. People desire community, yet are afraid of it. We need to concentrate in the *parish ministry on enabling our congregations to be true communities.* The Celtic Christians formed their communities successfully by living a rule of life, by being a *spiritual center,* a *learning center* and a *community center,* which often included training people for the ordained ministry for the larger community. They believed that God was present in such a community and they fostered a sense and belief in sacred space, especially where true community existed. They can be a model for us as we strive to become church communities in our time that are filled with God's presence and Spirit.

I am specifically speaking of the form of Christianity that developed primarily in Ireland, but in Wales and Scotland as well, in the fourth through ninth centuries C.E. It remained prevalent but altered in Ireland until the coming of the Normans, and the Christendom paradigm, in the twelfth century.

To speak of Celtic Christianity as a paradigm for the future is to walk on perilous ground. There are several prevalent misunderstandings concerning the Celtic Christians.

The first misunderstanding is that they developed independently from the Roman Catholic Church. There was no distinctive "Celtic Church" because the Celtic Christians always saw themselves as unified with Rome. It is proper to refer to them as "Celtic Christians" rather than as a "Celtic Church."[1] This misunderstanding about the Christian Celts developed at the turn of the century when English clerics debated whether a "Celtic Church" ever existed, a kind of pre-Reformation Church in the Anglican tradition.

Another misunderstanding concerns the word "Celtic." It does not refer to a basketball team in Boston and is pronounced with the "k" sound! The word "Celtic" began to be used to describe a linguistic family of languages by researchers in the eighteenth and nineteenth centuries. Linguists noticed a relationship between the languages and culture of Ireland, Scotland, Wales, Cornwall and Brittany and the Isle of Man. These languages came from a common cultural source. To describe this culture, they named it after one tribe of the culture, the *Keltos*. They referred to these languages as Celtic and these areas where Celtic Culture still existed as the "Celtic fringe." It is probable that the people we call "Celtic Christians" would not have thought of themselves as "Celts."[2]

The people we refer to today as "Celts" once covered much of Europe. They developed linguistically in the Hallstatt culture in modern Austria between 700 and 1000 B.C.E. This culture was followed by the LaTene culture. It was with these Celtic people that the Greeks and Romans first came in contact.[3] The Celtic people were not a unified culture or nation. They consisted of many diverse tribes. Each period of their his-

---

[1] Oliver Davies and Fiona Bowie, *Celtic Christian Spirituality: An Anthology of Medieval and Modern Sources* (New York: Continuum Publishing Company, 1995) 3.

[2] Ibid., 22.

[3] Ibid., 4.

tory and area of habitation are distinct within this "common" culture. They left no written word consequently all of their history, knowledge and stories were memorized by a priestly class, the *druids,* and by storytellers and poets, the *bards.*[4] Because of their tribal nature even their religion was a very local phenomenon, even in Christian times.[5] It is not known whether they conquered the people of Europe as they moved westward across the continent. It is more likely that they absorbed the Neolithic culture that existed before. Eventually they covered all of Europe except Rome and Greece. They moved into Britain and Ireland probably in about 300 B.C.E.[6]

A further truth about the Celts is that they were not part of the New Age movement or science fiction! We cannot use them to be culturally fashionable or different. We cannot use them to divorce ourselves from our culture. They were a distinct ancient culture that we know little about because it left no major cities, and no written record. The Celts eventually were conquered by the Romans and culturally absorbed by them.

This was true except in Ireland and parts of Scotland. The Roman legions never conquered these areas. "Ireland alone represents a Celtic tradition which was virtually untouched by *latinatics* and *romanatics,* which is to say the culture and civilization of the Roman empire," according to Celtic scholars Oliver Davies and Fiona Bowie.[7] In Wales and England the Romans lived with the Celtic people for over three hundred years. The Celtic culture became blended with the culture of Rome. In fact the word "Welsh" comes from an early English meaning "Romanized Celt." The Romans invaded Scotland but finally limited their penetration of the northern part of Britain at Hadrian's Wall. The Picts, the

[4] Simon James, *The World of the Celts* (London: Thames and Hudson, 1993) 53.

[5] Davies and Bowie, *Celtic Christian Spirituality,* 6.

[6] Thomas Cahill, *How the Irish Saved Civilization: The Untold Story of Ireland's Heroic Role from the Fall of Rome to the Rise of Medieval Europe* (New York: Doubleday) 231.

[7] Davies and Bowie, *Celtic Christian Spirituality,* 8.

people of Scotland were Celtic but a distinct kind of Celt from those in Ireland.[8]

The fact that Roman culture did not make it to Ireland is particularly helpful in looking for a new paradigm for ministry in our time. Because Roman culture was not present the early Christians there developed a model of ministry different than the model of the Apostolic or Christendom paradigms. They responded to their culture in a very distinct way. According to Kathleen Hughes and Ann Hamlin, two experts of Celtic Christianity, the Church in Ireland does not look the same because the Roman imperial armies did not reach there. The Church was never affected by Roman bureaucracy, law, building style or art.[9] The Christianity of the Celtic people of Ireland developed on its own even though they considered themselves part of the wider Church. This development was due to their relative isolation from the rest of the world, especially in Ireland. They developed things on their own. Examples are the issues of the monastic tonsure and the date of Easter, which were the topics of the discussion at the Synod of Whitby in 664 C.E. with Roman Christians.[10]

Because of their development outside of Rome maybe the faith of Celtic Christians can work as a guide for us as we develop a new way of living our faith as a response to our culture. We cannot make our churches like Celtic communities exclusively. We cannot make broad assumptions that Celtic Christians thought like we do; they did not, but we can look to them for ideas and a framework for doing mission and ministry in our time. To understand them and to develop our legitimate desire to find an alternative Christian model for today we must look at historical sources and archeological evidence of early Celtic Christianity. The communities of early Celtic Christianity are the only historical source I know of faith that developed outside of the sphere of Roman influence.

---

[8] Ibid.

[9] Kathleen Hughes and Ann Hamlin, *Celtic Monasticism: The Modern Traveler to the Early Irish Church* (New York: The Seabury Press, 1977) vii.

[10] Davies and Bowie, *Celtic Christian Spirituality,* 8.

What did Celtic Christians believe? What were Celtic Christian communities like? How can they serve as a guide for ministry in the parish today?

To understand how the Celtic Christians lived in community and to see how we can use their way of living as a model for the parish or congregation today, we have to first of all understand Celtic Christian spirituality.

Whenever we talk about the Celtic way of thinking we must be reminded of the circle. Everything in the Celtic mind was circular. Everything was connected. All reality has no beginning and no end. Time was irrelevant and there was no dividing line of history. There was also no division between the sacred and the secular, between God and the world. As in many religions the circle was the great symbol for the eternal.

The Celtic people inherited the idea of the circle from the spirituality of their ancestors. When they became Christians they incorporated much of what they believed as pagans into their Christian faith.

The most obvious example is the Celtic cross. The circle was the character of the cosmos. The universe and life went in a circular pattern. You began life and continued to live the circle until death and then life came again. The Celts could see this life cycle in the earth, in the heavens and in the seasons. In the Neolithic culture of Europe the worship of this universal force represented by the sun and the seasons was predominant.[11] The people constructed stone circles to represent this called "cromlechs." The most famous of these is Stonehenge, but there are about two hundred stone circles today surviving in Britain and Ireland.[12] The larger ones may have been used as huge astronomical observatories to watch the seasons. The smaller ones marked a sacred ritual space.[13] The circle represented the eternal cosmos to the early people of Europe and the Celts adopted this understanding. When

---

[11] Jacob Streit, *Sun and Cross: From Megalithic Culture to Early Christianity in Ireland* (Edinburgh: Floris Books, 1977) 20.

[12] Ibid., 21.

[13] Ibid.

Christianity came they adopted this symbol and they combined it with the cross. The circle behind the cross is a sign of this eternal truth in Christ. This innovation did not mean a breakdown in the Christian faith.[14] It shows how the faith of Christ was connected to what they believed before.[15]

This cross with a circle points to one of the elements of Celtic spirituality. The Celts had a circular understanding of time. Our culture looks upon time in a linear fashion. Events happen in time and we move toward a goal. The assumption is often made that the farther we go on this time line things will improve as we reach the goal. Events take place and are trapped in time. We can't go back. We can only go forward. We can only change the future. Celtic people believed time was continuous, like a circle, with no beginning or end. There was no division with the past or the future. Time was continually happening. There was no dividing line between mythology and history.[16] No separation from the past existed. If you lived in a place, for example, where a great saint had lived before, the saint still lived. There was no time division.

Because of this perspective the Celts were very tolerant when Christianity came. It appears that the Christian faith was accepted in Celtic lands without any violence.[17] That is why the pagan was so easily blended with Christian beliefs. This new world was the way things were; Christ was God and he would inevitably come; it was a natural "part" of the circle of time.

For this reason Christianity seems to always have been in Britain and Ireland. At least, it was there very early.

> "Legend tells us for instance, that Irish sages attended the events on Golgotha 'in the spirit' and felt by what means we cannot tell, 'the groans and travails of creation cease.'" Yeats notes a similar story in which on the day of

[14] Ibid., 124.

[15] Ibid., 111.

[16] Nigel Pennick, *Celtic Sacred Landscapes* (New York: Thames and Hudson, 1996) 7.

[17] Streit, *Sun and Cross,* 121.

Crucifixion King Conchubar and Bucrach the Leinster Druid are sitting together. Conchubar notices "the unusual changes of the creation and the eclipse of the sun and the moon at its full": he asks the Druid the cause of these signs and Bucrach replies, "Jesus Christ, the Son of God, who is now being crucified by the Jews."[18]

Other stories relate how the Irish saints Bridget and Ita were the nursemaids of Christ. To a Celtic person without a sense of linear time this was possible. When Bridget was too young to walk or talk she was cast adrift to the Holy Island of Iona. There she began to sing:

"I am but a little child,
Yet my mantle shall be laid
On the Lord of the World.
The King of the Elements Himself
Shall rest upon my heart,
and I will give Him Peace."[19]

Because of this time concept, Bridget also was connected with goddesses of the pagan world, Artemis of the Greeks and Bridghe of the Celts. If time is irrelevant then Bridget could nurse the Christ child, live in sixth-century Ireland, and be the goddess Bridghe at the same time. Time simply is not an issue in the Celtic mind.

Despite all of these stories Christianity was present in Britain and Ireland by 200 C.E. and in England St. Alban was martyred in 206 C.E. In 314 C.E., at the Council of Arles, three British bishops were present.[20]

Theologically the Celts believed in a "continuity in cosmic process that extended from its inception, creation, to its conclusion, deification." For the Celts, therefore, Christianity and the act of Christ was never an end in itself, but rather was

---

[18] Christopher Bamford and William Parker Marsh, *Celtic Christianity: Ecology and Holiness* (Great Barrington, Mass.: The Lindisfarne Press, 1987) 11.

[19] Ibid., 11.

[20] Ibid., 14.

always experienced as a divine means to the true end.[21] Christ was part of the divine plan for the creation which included all spirituality. This could be a guide for us in our evangelism as we respect other religious traditions and at the same time tell people the Gospel message.

Because of this spirituality of time the Celts had no trouble believing in the communion of saints as this beautiful poem attributed to Bridget reveals.[22]

THE HEAVENLY BANQUET

I would like to have the men of Heaven
In my own house:
With vats of good cheer
Laid out for them.

I would like to have the three Marys,
Their fame is so great.
I would like people
From every corner of Heaven.

I would like them to be cheerful
In their drinking,
I would like to have Jesus too
Here amongst them.

I would like a great lake of beer
For the King of Kings,
I would like to be watching Heaven's family
Drinking it through all eternity.

Another element of Celtic Christian Spirituality is the idea of the spiritual life as a journey. Life in Christ is like a journey with no momentum: we are always at the beginning. We can see this theme vividly in the "knots" of Celtic art. The knots or interlacing in much of Celtic art appears to be simply interlocked but if you look closely they are interlocked circles. They symbolize the moving in and out of life, going in different directions but always looking for and arriving at the same end.

[21] Ibid., 12–13.
[22] A. M. Allchin and Esther de Waal, eds., *Daily Readings from Prayers and Praises in the Celtic Tradition* (Springfield, Illinois: Templegate Publishers, 1986) 58.

Life in God is to always be searching never quite being content until we arrive at the end in the Heart of God. Spirals in Celtic art also symbolize this mystical path to God. They indicate the way of contemplation of the spiritual path. The spiral sweeps from the infinite to the finite or vice versa.[23]

This is a great spiritual insight. God is not through with us yet. God is always forming us as we go through life making us into the person we are meant to be. The Celts also believed in life that they could somewhat affect their own salvation. Pelagius was probably from Wales, named Morgan, and was the first British Christian to write a book. He was expelled as a heretic in 412 C.E. for his beliefs. The Irish would have believed with Pelaguis that "since perfection is possible for man it is obligatory." They would not agree that human free will could do this unaided. They believed that it was only by the gift of grace from God that this could be accomplished. "The Irish believed in a healthy interdependence of nature and grace."[24]

Because Celtic Christians believed what they did in life affected their salvation they were highly penitential. On the earthly journey or pilgrimage you did penance for the wrongs you had done. To them it was a positive action; it involved not just the mind but the body in the spiritual life. They fasted often, spent long periods of time in prayer, and did the "cross vigil," a prayer while the arms were outstretched like Christ on the cross. The Celtic Christians also often took a vow of poverty as penance. All of this active penance in life was helpful in the spiritual journey.

The Celtic Christians also took the image of spiritual journey literally; they went on pilgrimages far and wide. They were also very evangelical in the process; they told other people about Christ on the way. This was the case with two famous Celtic missionaries, Columcille or Columba, and Columbanus.

They seemed to have been embarrassed by the fact there were no martyrs in the Christianizing of Ireland. If you effectively "witnessed" to Christ you would die for the faith. But

---

[23] Streit, *Sun and Cross,* 51.
[24] Bamford and Marsh, *Celtic Christianity,* 17.

it didn't happen, at least until the Vikings arrived. The Celtic Christians invented three kinds of martyrdom. Red martyrdom was witness by death for the faith. Green martyrdom meant freeing one's self from desires by fasting, labor, and prayer. It was showing your belief by lifestyle. White martyrdom was the purest form of witness besides death. It meant abandoning everything you love for the faith in God. There is a famous poem by Columba who left his home in Derry, Ireland, for Scotland lamenting the loss of his life in white martyrdom.[25]

> Great is the speed of my coracle,
> And its stern turned upon Derry;
> Grievous is my errand over the main,
> Travelling to Alba of the beetling brows.
>
> Were all Alba mine
> From its centre to its border,
> I would rather have the site of a house
> In the middle of fair Derry.
>
> It is for this I love Derry,
> For its smoothness, for its purity;
> All full of angels
> Is every leaf on the oaks of Derry.
>
> My Derry, my little oak-grove,
> My dwelling and my little cell,
> O living God that art in Heaven above,
> Woe to him who violates it!

It was seeking white martyrdom that led the great Celtic missionaries on their evangelistic journeys. The most spiritual manner was to put your whole trust in God for the journey. Monks would cast off into the ocean in their tiny boats made a wood frame covered with hides. They would have no oars and would put their trust in God. The Venerable Bede tells us of some Irish monks who sailed off and landed in Cornwall. When brought to the king and asked to explain themselves they said, "we stole away because we wanted for

[25] De Waal, *The Celtic Way of Prayer,* 12.

the love of God to be on pilgrimage, we cared not where."[26] A famous Celtic saint, St. Brendan, probably went on his famous voyage for this reason.

But the real journey in the spiritual life is in the heart. One way of going on the spiritual journey was to stay in one place. If you loved God then you already had Christ with you. To really be on a journey with Christ he must already hold a place in our lives. The following poem illustrates:

> To go to Rome
> Is much of trouble, little of profit;
> The King whom thou seekest
> Unless thou bring Him with Thee,
> Thou wilt not find.[27]

The Celtic Christians tied the two ideas, pilgrimage and penance, together by going off in solitude. They purged themselves of all they loved in white martyrdom and lived an ascetical lifestyle in green martyrdom. These hermits often attracted others by their holiness; however, hermits started many communities such as Glendalough and Clonmacnois in Ireland. All of these travelers were looking for the "place of resurrection." This place was where they eventually died but it was more. It was the place where a person could become the person they might hope to be, the true self in Christ.[28] This was the place we all hope to find. It is the end of the spiritual journey but also the beginning.

The Celts also believed this place to be literal. Another element of Celtic spirituality, connected to the rest, is a belief in the presence of God in the world. God is not far off. God is here in creation. The incarnation of Christ makes the truth even more vivid.

The early Celts, like the later Celtic Christians, believed the spiritual world was simply a step away. It was not necessarily

---

[26] Esther de Waal, *A World Made Whole: Rediscovering the Celtic Tradition* (London: Harper Collins, 1991) 19.

[27] De Waal, *The Celtic Way of Prayer*, 10.

[28] Ibid., 2.

seen but it was here and its presence could be sensed. Just a
movement away, right next to you was the place where all
people went after death, *Tir-na-gog,* the land of eternal summer. This place is the dream of all who live in my climate of
North America. It is a place where it is always summer in full
bloom like the first warm day when the lilacs are blooming.
This land was in the west, out somewhere in the ocean because the people of Ireland knew of no land after that shore.
It was *Tir-na-gog* that St. Brendan was looking for when he
sailed away in search of paradise. Even today in Ireland when
someone dies it is referred to as "he sailed" or "had a good
crossing." This phase refers to the setting of the sun in the
west, the Land of the Dead. In the timeless mind of the Celt
all people were still alive, present in this place.[29]

We are often guilty of separating God from the earth, thinking that spiritual things are not of this world. We think of
spiritual people as not being very human but having the usual
failings. To Celtic Christians ordinary life is sacred. There are
Celtic prayers for everything from banking the fire at night to
milking the cow to saying a morning prayer as you awake.
Celtic Christianity, for all its "pagan" elements is very orthodox. There is no division of the Trinity into three separate
persons that have no relationship to the other two. The presence of God is always mentioned as the Trinity. God is one in
Trinity of Persons. Because God is always present Celtic spirituality is highly contemplative. The Prayer of Remembrance,
when we remember the presence of God, is commonly used.
Whenever we simply sit in contemplation and remember God,
the Deity is there. A beautiful poem by the contemporary
Welsh poet R. S. Thomas, who was a priest in the Church in
Wales, will illustrate:[30]

THE BRIGHT FIELD

I have seen the sun break through
to illuminate a small field

[29] Streit, *Sun and Cross.*
[30] R. S. Thomas, *Poems of R. S. Thomas* (Fayetteville, Ark.: The University of Arkansas Press, 1985) 104.

for a while, and gone my way
and forgotten it. But that was the pearl
of great price, the one field that had
the treasure in it. I realize now
that I must give all that I have
to possess it. Life is not hurrying
on to a receding future, nor hankering after
an imagined past. It is the turning
aside like Moses to the miracle
of the lit bush, to a brightness
that seemed as transitory as your youth
once, but is the eternity that awaits you.[31]

Because God is present in the world the creation is sacred. This is something we have lost in the Enlightenment and our separation from God in our culture. In the belief of the early Celts the Sun created the earth each season so it was sacred. In Christianity God, the Creator, also continues to create in Christ and the Holy Spirit. Each part of creation is holy. The Celtic Christians were not pantheists; they did not worship rocks and trees as gods, even though that is how the belief of the pagan Celts was perceived. They and their pagan ancestors were panentheists; they saw God in creation; the Creator God was visible in the earth and its creatures. Each created thing had a purpose and story, a reason for its existence and location.[32] If you looked at the rocks on the shore of a lake, for example, each one had a name and a reason for being there. You were connected with these rocks and their story by the fact that you were there. Every object and creature on earth is interconnected and comes from God and reveals the Creator.

Each part of the Celtic landscape has a history and a purpose, too. If you travel in the Celtic lands you will notice that there is a name and story for each hill, stream, lake, valley, and mountain. Each place has a part in the sacred.

[31] Reprinted by permission of the University of Arkansas Press. Copyright 1975 by R. S. Thomas.
[32] Pennick, *Celtic Sacred Landscapes,* 8.

There are especially sacred spots or locations. Dr. George MacLeod, founder of the Iona Community, has referred to these places as "thin spots." These thin places are "where the membrane between this world and the other world, between the material and the spiritual was very permeable." The author Phillip Sheldrake puts it this way:

> Celtic Christians had—and even today have—a strong sense of living on "edges" or "boundary places" between the material world and the other world. The natural landscape was both a concrete reality where people lived and, at the same time, a doorway into another spiritual world.[33]

These "thin places" are perceived mostly on "edges" of the landscape where there is a literal boundary between worlds. Wells are sacred because they open up into the earth. Rivers and waterfalls are sacred because water runs with life and divides the land. Cliffs and shores and mountains are sacred boundaries. Mountains are connected and a border to the sky. The ocean is another world, and especially beneath the waters, the very surface of a lake, pond, ocean, or river is sacred. Trees connect to the earth and to under the ground so that they are thin points. Animals, especially fish, otters, and birds, are sacred because they live in two worlds and constantly cross an "edge."

The belief in thin places probably comes again from Neolithic beliefs in Europe that were adopted by the Celts. The early inhabitants of Europe erected "standing stones," stones that can still be seen on the landscapes of Europe and especially Britain and Ireland. These are called *menhirs*. "Whenever a menhir rises it indicates an earthly centre where the lower, earth and man, can link with higher, with the cosmos and the gods."[34] Standing stones are the symbols of a sacred point in

---

[33] Phillip Sheldrake, *Living Between Worlds: Place and Journey in Celtic Spirituality* (Cambridge and Boston: Cowley Publications, 1995) 7.
[34] Streit, *Sun and Cross,* 12.

the landscape. Later in Christian Ireland, for instance, they were marked with crosses making them Christian sacred places. New high crosses were erected to mark sacred ground.[35] Round towers, often the most noticeable part of a Celtic religious community remaining in Ireland, were erected to mark a spiritual place, connecting it with the vertical dimension.

These beliefs may seem like magic to our twenty-first-century minds trained on science and Enlightenment philosophy. Yet we know we need to rediscover the sacred presence in the earth and ourselves. By the grace of God in the Holy Spirit we can be the Body of Christ in the world. We can experience the sacred. In our spiritual journey we are looking for a sacred place, a place and time when we can be healthy and whole, a "place of resurrection."

The understanding of "thin spots" is inherent in the Celtic mind and is still carried by people in the Celtic "fringe" as well as their relations. I am of Irish and Welsh ancestry and I can acutely feel the presence of God in certain places and feel the presence of people who have been there before.

When in Wales on a pilgrimage I noticed another member of our party picking up small stones carefully wherever she went. She would also reverently place another stone from her pocket and leave it whenever she went to a sacred place. I finally asked her to explain. She said her Irish grandmother had introduced her to the practice. "Irish people take a stone from one holy place and bring it home as a holy relic. They leave a stone from home in its place. It's what we do," she said. Everything is interconnected and has a story. Everything is part of a great circle. In a way this circle is the ultimate community. Every created thing is part of this cosmic community in God.

Another element of Celtic spirituality, which is interconnected with all the other aspects of this spirituality, was the sense of family. For Celtic people their family and clan were all important. Like the Jews they were very proud of their genealogy and carefully memorized their lineage. They lived in a very

[35] Pennick, *Celtic Sacred Landscapes,* 166.

rural world. There were no roads, as we know them. When you left your family and kin you were in the wilderness. When you journeyed from their territory you could be in hostile ground. Without clan and family you had no identity.

Celtic Christianity received much of its Christian theology from the Desert Fathers and Mothers. The spirituality of the desert of St. Anthony of Egypt traveled from Egypt with John Cassian (d. 435 C.E.) and was taken by St. Martin of Tours when he established his community in Gaul in the fourth century C.E. The ascetical, penitential practices of the desert appealed to Celtic Christians. Their spirit of contemplation, solitude, and spiritual journeys were similar. They both lived outside of the cities and urban Greco-Roman influence. They shared the same type of mystical wisdom. Desert spirituality was also monastic and Celtic spirituality was monastic too. It was centered in a monastic community.

People in early Celtic times lived in an extended family or clan called the *tuath*. At the head of each *tuath* was a king or *ri* whose stature came from the *fine,* the larger extended family or tribe. Ranked below the *ri* were noble kinspeople, the learned class, the lawmakers, the bards who guarded the traditions, stories, and genealogies of the tribe, and the druids, the priests of the pagan Celts. Finally, the family contained warriors, laborers, tradesmen, and slaves. A high king or *ruir,* great king, ruled over all of these extended families. Each family unit lived in a circular hill fort, surrounded by a circle of banks and ditches, and a wall called a *dun* or *rath,* a hill fort.[36]

Monasticism formed the core of the Irish church when Christianity came to Ireland and to other areas of Britain. It centered around the family. When you became a Christian you became part of a monastic family, monastic in name only, because you were set apart from greater society. You were part of the family of the founding saint and often the monastic community was built on tribal land. These communities were surrounded by symbolic circular walls and ditched like the

---

[36] John Marsden, *Sea Road of the Saints: Celtic Holy Men in the Hebrides* (Edinburgh: Floris Books, 1995) 26–27.

raths or duns. But this circle was different. It was a spiritual community, part of the interconnected relationship of all things in Christ. This Christian community was sacred ground. It carried with it all the circular elements of Celtic spirituality but most importantly the early Celtic Christian communities were thin spots, in the circle the sacred world and the material world were one. The kingdom of God, or the fulfillment of God, was present in community; in fact, God was present in their midst.

It is this theology of the presence of God in the world and interconnectedness of all things that we need in our time. We especially need to know that our activities make a difference in bringing about what God wants in the world. The idea of the community as dwelling place of God is the model we need to bring to our congregations today. We need to celebrate our congregations' communities where God is truly present. Our churches are "thin spots" where people acutely feel and see the presence of God. Celtic Christian communities are a model for us to follow in ministry as we respond to our individualistic culture.

What were Celtic communities like? Celtic Christians carried this idea of sacred space, thin spots, and edges to its fullest extent in their communities. They believed the sacred and the secular were not separate on earth and that in their community heaven was joined to earth. This was especially true in the case of the sacred circle. They believed that by drawing a circle, imagining a circle, or building a circle they could make sacred space. They called this *Caim* (rhymes with time and begins with a "k" sound as in Celt), or the encirclement or encompassing. "In times of danger people would draw a circle around themselves with the index finger of the right hand. They would point and turn around sun-wise, praying to the Trinity to encircle and protect them."[37] Apparently Celtic people used these *Caim* prayers from ancient pagan times consistent with their belief in the spirituality of the circle. We can find many examples of Celtic Christians using the *Caim*.

[37] Sheldrake, *Living Between Worlds,* 9–10.

A delightful example is from St. Aelred's *Life of St. Ninian,* a biography of one of the earliest Celtic Saints.

> The most holy Ninian liked to visit herds and the huts of his shepherds desiring that the flocks which were kept for the use of the brethren and the poor should partake of the episcopal blessing. And so, the animals having been brought together in one place, when the servant of the Lord (Ninian) had looked upon them with uplifted hands he commended himself and all of his to divine protection. Then walking around them all and as it were drawing a circle with his staff on which he leant, he confided all within that enclosure to peaceful rest throughout the night under divine protection.[38]

Alexander Carmichael collected many *Caim* prayers in the Outer Hebrides at the end of the nineteenth century when they were still in common use.[39]

A well-known encirclement prayer is the famous lorica or breastplate of St. Patrick that Episcopalians often sing as a hymn at ordinations or in celebration of the Trinity.

It was natural that Celtic Christians would mark their communities with the *Caim* circle to make them sacred Christian spaces. Monks would use elaborate rituals to mark sacred enclosures and surround them with circular walls. They would first mark them with spades as they said a blessing. Then they would find the spiritual center of the enclosure. They would then arrange the space into divisions like a target with the most sacred area in the center.[40] By the eighth century C.E. they had actually prescribed the rules for enclosing a sacred area in this manner.[41] This was such a natural part of the Celtic culture that the Celtic Christians would never build a community in

---

[38] David Keller, *"Caim Spring Newsletter,"* vol.1, no.1, p. 2.

[39] Alexander Carmichael, *Carmina Gadelica* (Hudson, New York: Lindisfarne Press, 1992).

[40] Lisa M. Bitel, *Isle of the Saints: Monastic Settlement and Christian Community in Early Ireland* (Ithaca, New York: Cornell University Press, 1960) 61.

[41] Ibid., 66.

any other way. When St. Malachy tried to convince the monks of Armagh to build a rectangular cloister they replied *Scottis summus non galli,* "We're Irish, not Gauls!" After the Normans conquered Ireland they tried to bring the Benedictine cloister to Ireland but with limited success at first. When a Cistercian abbot visitor came to Ireland on an inspection in the mid-thirteenth century C.E. he found that monks in one monastery had built the stone cloisters to satisfy the rules of the order but had abandoned them for the traditional wattle huts that formally were inside the circular enclosures.[42]

To the Irish the circular enclosure was a replica of the cosmos, "an attempt to create a place that existed simultaneously on this earthly plane and on the eternal plane."[43] As Phillip Sheldrake puts it "such places were replicas of the cosmos, microcosms of the macrocosm."[44] This was a place where secular and sacred met, therefore it was a place where religious and cultural dialogue took place. As mentioned earlier, the circular enclosure was sacred space. The intent was that when you entered into the circle you were entering into a space where God truly entered the earth. Every action in life inside the circle had to be as God intended.

The center of the circle was where the relics of a saint were kept, usually the remains of the founding saint of the community. Where the saint's bones rested, as in their lifetime, sanctity was near. The saint was still there in the great circle of time to protect and guide the community. The walls were marked as sacred with stone crosses. Round towers marked the sacred community and could be seen far away. Like the great standing stones they were a symbol that heaven and earth met in this place. "The monastery's walls and markers sent a message across the Christian landscape, which still echoes today among monastic ruins: the Saint dwells here with the monks."[45]

---

[42] Ibid., 17.
[43] Ibid., 61.
[44] Sheldrake, *Living Between Worlds,* 34.
[45] Bitel, *Isle of the Saints,* 37.

Inside the circular walls the community tried to fulfill the kingdom of God. The center of the circle where the saints' relics were kept was called the *termonn* (from the Latin *terminus*). This was holy ground where prayers were said and the Eucharist celebrated. Often this space was restricted to those in orders or who had vowed a strict monastic rule. This retreat was a place of peace: refugees fled there. No violence could be done in this place. The transitional area between the most sacred area of the church was called the *platea* or courtyard. It was where liturgy and ceremonies often occurred.[46]

The vision Christians have of a world where everything is as God intends for it to be is often called the kingdom of God, a world where God reigns. In this kingdom every person is included. This was the case in Celtic Christian communities. Some monks lived with their families in the enclosure. Other people lived in the enclosure or just outside of it and did chores or were skilled workers for the community.[47] Some communities had both men and women in monastic orders. The abbot could be either a man or a woman. St. Bridget and St. Hilda of Whitby are notable examples. Inside the walls the people joined together in their words as a "familia."[48]

Because the presence of God is here on earth and especially represented by the community in the sacred enclosure, the people living there had constant business with the world outside the walls. The circular walls were most often only symbolic; they were not designed like later monastic communities, to keep the world outside. There was often a creative tension between the "desire for seclusion and the wish to be accessible and open to society at large."[49] Sites for monastic enclosures were often chosen because they were places where ordinary people already gathered. They were places that offered seclusion as well as access.[50] Often they were already sacred places

---

[46] Ibid., 73–76.
[47] Ibid., 80.
[48] Ibid., 88.
[49] Sheldrake, *Living Between Worlds*, 31.
[50] Ibid., 23.

to the pagan Celts such as Derry with its sacred oak groves or Kildare that means "Church of the Oak."

They often were places where sacred "edges" were most present. They were "thin spots" already. Skellig Michael, off the southwest coast of Ireland, is a mountain island surrounded by water. Clonmacnois is in the center of Ireland literally at the crossroads. Glendalough is in a beautiful valley with two lakes. Pennant Melangell in Wales is in a similar valley with a stream flowing through it with a waterfall. Nendrum in Ireland is at the mouth of a river where it meets the ocean. All of these places are sacred in the eyes of the Celtic people.

Sometimes they were on the borders of clan lands or earthly kingdoms, another edge.[51] But, often they were related to the surrounding family. When a person became a committed member of a Christian community they left their genealogical clan for a Christian one: they left the family circular *dun* or hill fort for the sacred circular enclosure.[52] In some cases the ring fort and the sacred enclosure coexisted on the same site.[53]

It seems that everyone in the area of the sacred enclosure was connected with the monastic community. In exchange for labor and skills from the outside people the monks prayed. Those people who were not members of the celibate monastic order were regarded as clients of the saint and had a semi-religious status.[54] The hagiographies, the stories of the saints, show that these people were protected by the saint and the sacred circular enclosure of the Christian community. It was as if God and the founding saints were saying "harass monastic clients at your peril."[55]

Celtic monastic communities were more like modern day congregations than the monasteries that became dominant in Europe during the Middle Ages. They were spiritual centers

[51] Ibid., 29–30.
[52] Bitel, *Isle of the Saints,* 86–88.
[53] Sheldrake, *Living Between Worlds,* 29.
[54] Bitel, *Isle of the Saints,*124.
[55] Ibid., 125.

where the people gathered for prayer and worship and to hear the Gospels read. The clients of the community often were trained to read and help with worship.[56]

The Celtic Christian monastic communities also served as huge community centers with many programs going on simultaneously. With the idea of the communities being a place of sanctuary from violence they often served more as prisons.[57] When the monks offered hospitality to prisoners, criminals became penitents and either joined the community or dealt with the results of their crimes outside the walls. Communities also served as hotels offering hospitality to travelers. Successful communities often were built by major routes of travel for this purpose.[58] Monasteries also served as banks where valuable items could be kept safe from theft, or as a pledge to complete a business deal.[59] They also functioned as universities, training places for law, or the religious life replacing the pagan druids and bards. Many of the great saints were trained in the "seminaries" of the larger communities.

The sacred enclosure was where the kingdom, the sacred, met the ordinary things of life. But, consistent with Celtic belief of the presence of God, all of life and everyone in proximity of the community was accepted. Each person was accepted for what they were. Kathleen Hughes says "Irish monasticism accepted that men had different gifts and different capacities and God did not call them all to the same degree of discipline."[60] All people were accepted and possibly lived different "rules" as they were attached to the community. Both sexes were considered "monks" even though they may have lived a normal family life.[61]

Most important Celtic monastic communities were places of vision where a different world, the world intended by God, could be lived out. All people were created to live in relation-

---

[56] Sheldrake, *Living Between Worlds,* 16.
[57] Ibid., 126.
[58] Hughes and Hamlin, *Celtic Monasticism,* 15.
[59] Ibid., 13.
[60] Ibid., 2.
[61] Sheldrake, *Living Between Worlds,* 39.

ship with God. They became *learning centers, community centers,* and *spiritual centers* for the people of God. All people were asked to be part of the monastic community. They were attempts at living in true community with God present in their midst.[62]

Celtic communities literally believed this was true. A Celtic motto puts it this way:

> The People
> The Pastor
> The Place.
> Shall be as one
> In the service
> Of Christ.[63]

A. M. Allchin tells this wonderful story from the annals of the Celtic community of Landevennec in Brittany:[64]

> [There] are places whose power persists through centuries of indifference and neglect to be revealed again when men are ready for it, places which display the potential holiness of all this earth which man has loved so much, yet so much ravaged.
>
> One such place is to be found at the furthest tip of Brittany, Landevennec, in the early period of the Celtic Church a great centre of light and learning, then for long centuries in eclipse, finally destroyed at the time of the French revolution only to come to new life within our own generation. The monastery is placed as many monasteries are, in a situation of outstanding natural beauty. . . .
>
> "It is a kind of Paradise prepared by God for his servants, and as it is rich in the fruits of the earth, so it is rich in heavenly fruits." The writer tells us how at the beginning of the community's life in the time of the founder, it was discovered that none of the monks could

---

[62] Ibid., 39.

[63] *The Book of Escomb: Prayers in the Escomb Tradition* (London: Nicolas Deddow) 31.

[64] A. M. Allchin, *The World Is a Wedding* (New York: Oxford University Press, 1978) 21.

die, even though they suffered the infirmities of old age. "The oldest of the brethren, burdened by the weight of many years longed to be dissolved and released from this crumbling frame of clay." The reason why this was so was finally revealed. In a vision the brethren saw an opening in heaven above the monastery exactly the size of the monastery itself, and the angels of God ascending and descending. The correspondence of earth and heaven, of time and eternity was so exact, that here on earth time seemed to have come to a stop. The brethren exhorted their abbot to pull down the buildings and to move a little nearer to the shore. And this they did. Even this slight removal secured the desired effect. It became possible to die, but only from old age; and for a long time the writer assures us that the brethren died only in strict order of seniority. "And this was long the rule in the monastery and has only recently been changed."

The monks of Landevennec literally believed their enclosure was a spot where heaven and earth were linked. The two had become one in true community and living out the kingdom of God. Celtic communities were not perfect; there are examples of how they failed in this vision in all the stories of the saints and their communities.[65] The ideal and intent of their communities was to live as close to what God intended in true community. The symbol, but literal sign of this vision, was the sacred circles the enclosure of the community. It was in the circle that the kingdom reigned in community.

My thesis is that the ways of the early Celtic Christian communities can be used as a model for parish ministry today. Our churches should strive to be true communities where God is most evident in the lives of the people and their relationships. This community spills outside of the walls of the church building to affect the surrounding community. Congregations should work to become *spiritual centers* where prayer occurs and is taught. They should be *learning centers* for training in mission

[65] Ard Macha, or Armagh was burned, raided, or violated in some way fifty times between 800–1200 C.E. says Bitel, *Isle of the Saints,* 148.

and ministry. They could become *outreach centers* for service and evangelism. Most important, they should be seen as places where heaven and earth meet, as "places" where the presence of God is acutely felt.

It is in this way that congregations can meet the challenges of ministry today in our culture and grow as healthy church communities. They can meet the challenge of individuality and provide community in people's lives.

The local congregation is where ministry will be centered in the next century. They must grow as community centers and spiritual centers where the incarnation of Christ is perceived.

People in our time are not hostile to the Church as they were in the apostolic era. They also are not universally considered part of the Church as in the Christendom era. These paradigms of looking at the Church are no longer true. Most people are indifferent to the Church. They see Church as irrelevant to their lives. "What difference does it make in my life?" they say. The local congregation is where the difference will be made.

The Christian communities in Celtic Ireland, Scotland, and Wales were up against many of the same conditions as today. When the Romans left Britain early in the fifth century C.E., after four hundred years of occupation, their society changed rapidly. People began to move into Britain who were not Christian or Celtic. Life was chaotic. In Celtic lands people accepted great diversity in religion. After all, every religion and belief is part of the great circle. People were tolerant of the beliefs and pagans often lived alongside Christian communities.[66] With all the change in Britain people had to adjust to diversity and new culture. In Ireland the Church had to show that it was different and relevant in people's lives. It had to face the diversity, go to the people, and use the culture to teach the faith and evangelize.[67] There were no martyrs in the Christianizing of Ireland. People had to be witnesses in new ways, by their lifestyle and their commitment to living as a Christian rather than their untimely death.

[66] Bitel, *Isle of the Saints,* 142.
[67] Sheldrake, *Living Between Worlds,* 29.

We have the same challenge in our culture in a much different time. Our culture is becoming more and more diverse. There is a tolerance for all religions and no longer do most people believe that Christianity has all the answers to life's questions. Individualism has caused our society to be less communal and more fragmented. People are in desperate need of community in spite of being afraid or unaware of it. The Church can provide community, but it also must go to where the people are and adjust to the culture without giving up essential beliefs. They must exhibit all the healthy signs of true community. They must be inclusive, realistic, contemplative communities who heal, convert, and show the Spirit of God. If the churches show these qualities people will see that they are different, but relevant to life as well. Most important the churches and congregations must be seen as sacred places where heaven and earth meet. They must be seen as centers of prayer, worship, and especially compassion.

The early Celtic Christian communities can be a model for us as we develop a new paradigm for parish ministry in our time. They can provide an example of how they responded to a culture that was not Greco-Roman. They can provide examples of true communities serving as centers for ministry, education, spirituality, and outreach. Loren Mead presents an ideal image of congregations in the next century in his book *More Than Numbers: The Ways Churches Grow*. He says they must grow in other ways besides membership. These ways of growth seem to parallel the Celtic Christian model of community.

First of all, Mead says we have to deal with a variety of commitments to the church. Many people have a peripheral attachment to the church but are deeply touched by the church in life transitions like marriage, funerals, and baptisms.[68] Often these people are easily dropped from the church roles when the parish list is gleaned by a new pastor or a cost conscious church board who wants to cut down on mailings. We

[68] Loren B. Mead, *More Than Numbers: The Ways Churches Grow* (Washington, D.C.: The Alban Institute, 1993) 14–15.

must see our ministry to all the people around us, who are called to be in relationship with God.

Next, congregations must be places that train "professional" class teachers, leaders, and administrators. "The only institution that can produce ministry for the twenty-first century is the congregation. It is the only institution that can do for the next century what seminaries have done for the last one—produce ministers."[69]

The effective congregation of the next century must provide an overall curriculum containing the biblical story, working theologies, world realities, ethics, stewardship, land use and environment, new perspectives in career, and practical theology.[70] In this institution the senior minister serves as dean of the seminary. He or she makes sure the community of learning is built up and the curriculum in place seeks faculty members. In the words of Mead, the minister "makes sure the fabric is intact and occasionally teaches a course that is a personal specialty."[71] The courses offered cover a scope of needs from beginners to advanced learners. This vision seems very similar to the role of many of the larger Celtic communities that offered free education to anyone. The role of the new Minister Dean, seems similar to one of the roles of the abbot in Celtic communities.

All of this training shifts from ministry to the people inside the church to those outside the church. It is the role of the trained, ordained clergy to conduct this shift. This changes how we currently train clergy. People need to be trained to have dialogue with God. "How can I change?" must be the question asked.[72] Theology and ministry must be relevant in people's lives inside and outside of the church.

A church must have spiritual directors who are trained and available as needed. Good worship is vital. Skilled help must be available for help at transitional points in people's lives. A

---

[69] Ibid., 44.
[70] Ibid., 45.
[71] Ibid., 46.
[72] Ibid., 51.

constant spiritual path must be laid out for people that deals with life's complexities.[73] New members need training and knowledge of what is expected in membership. Many of them do not know the Faith.[74] All of this sounds similar to the role of soul friends in Celtic communities who served as mentors and spiritual directors for all sorts of people.

Besides being an educational center for the larger community in ministry and spirituality the local congregation must also "match its behavior with its values and beliefs,"[75] Mead says. In other words: it must be a true community reaching out to others. The temptations are to reconstruct the old Christendom Empire by building a "Christian" version of a just society, establishing a religious-secular coalition with the "right" persons in power, or making the church a universal holy club. Congregations must be true communities that include everyone "as bases where ministry is done."[76]

When the congregation exhibits this community the congregation will grow incarnationally. They will show people that Jesus did come as God into the world and that the Church is the Body of Christ in the world God is alive in Christ and makes all the difference in the world. The Church is the ultimate reality and relevancy in people's lives. It shows Christ. Mead says that the quality of community must be restored to congregations before this kind of incarnational growth can occur. The presence of community is central.[77]

The vision of a longtime expert in congregational development, Loren Mead, and myself looks very similar to the vision of the early communities of Celtic Christians. They served as training centers for ministry, reached out in relevant ministry in people's lives, and served as spiritual centers of worship and prayer. They strived to be the place where incarnational growth was present. They were the place where the saints dwelled, Christ lived, and heaven met the earth.

[73] Ibid., 53–56.
[74] Ibid., 27–29.
[75] Ibid., 73.
[76] Ibid., 96–99.
[77] Ibid., 101–02.

An example of a congregation that has held the vision of community is the congregation I have served, Ascension Episcopal Church in Stillwater, Minnesota. The fabric of everything in the parish is woven according to this vision of God in community. Often the congregation falls short of the vision of being contemplative, realistic, and a place where people are healed and converted but begin over and over again. In several recent surveys the people of Ascension Church said that community was the main quality of their congregation.[78] When I was interviewed as rector, one of their major goals was to grow as a community. The other goals related to more education and outreach ministry and to being better stewards of resources for ministry. Their vision was similar to Loren Mead's vision of congregations in the twenty-first century.

The Church of the Ascension, in many ways, is a typical suburban church in our time apart from having a long history. Many people in Stillwater do not consider themselves suburban at all; Stillwater existed years before the nearby large cities of Minneapolis and St. Paul. Stillwater was the first community of white settlers on the Minnesota frontier in 1843. The Church of the Ascension was officially formed in 1846, ten years before the Diocese of Minnesota. Services were held in Stillwater as early as 1837. James Lloyd Breck and Jackson Kemper, two people remembered in the Lesser Feasts of the Episcopal Church, were involved in Ascension Church's early years. With all of their history people at Ascension Church feel rooted here. In a survey in 1995, 98 percent of the members said they did not want to move from their present building, built in 1888, to a new one. The resistance came not from worshiping the building but from considering the place with such history as sacred ground.

The challenges and problems of Ascension Church are common suburban issues for churches in our time. There is rapid population growth in the Stillwater area. The church has grown almost 100 percent in the last five years in membership. The population consists mainly of young families with

---

[78] In 1991 and 1995 surveys were conducted.

children and baby boomers. All of the consumer, individualistic, and media oriented issues of our time prevail. According to a demographic study of the area people were most interested in personal spiritual growth, family issues such as parenting and caring for aged parents, and daycare. They were concerned about jobs, money, and relieving stress.[79]

A guide to establishing programs to meet these interests can come from the work of Tex Sample who says that from his studies three distinct cultural lifestyles exist in the United States, the "cultural right, left, and middle." The cultural right are blue-collar, "hard-living" people, the culture shown mainly in country-western music. The cultural left are those who tend to be most liberal, individualistic, and tolerant of diversity. They are the "New Age" people, a large percentage of whom are baby boomers who grew up in the "'60s." The cultural middle are the more conservative, "culturally correct" people who are the successful bankers, lawyers, doctors, scientists, and business people in corporate and small businesses. The cultural left believes in diversity, tolerance, imagination, and spiritual journey. The cultural middle relates to problem solving, intellectual questioning, and education.[80]

Ascension Church is made up, almost exclusively of cultural left and middle people. There are very few, if any, members of the cultural right. The idea of a diverse community appeals to the cultural left baby boomers of the congregation. Life to them is a spiritual journey with no beginning or end. They relate to the Celtic idea of the circle. The cultural middle people enjoy courses that speak to their questioning and desire for relevant theology. Both positions are hungry for the feeling of spirit in community.

In this suburban climate which is challenged more and more by growth and diversity I believe community can grow and

[79] Percept Ministry Area Profile. September 1995, prepared by Percept, Costa Mesa, California.

[80] Tex Sample, *U.S. Lifestyles and Mainline Churches: A Key to Reaching People in the 90's* (Louisville, Kentucky: Westminster/John Knox Press, 1990) 25–122.

relevant ministry can occur. The church can become a spiritual center of faith, education, and ministry, as I envision it, modeled by the early Celtic Christian communities.

It is in the idea of a rule of life that has been the center of ministry and development of community at Ascension Church, following the model of the Celtic Christians. The living of a rule of life assists and supports the manifestation of authentic community. It serves as a guide for people and the parish as a whole to evaluate how well we are living as a real community. Having a rule of life enables people to see themselves as being different, being able to pray, grow, and work in the world in ways that make a difference because they are done with God. It is the living of a rule of life in the parish and the affect that it has on people's lives that supports my thesis that our parishes need to be true communities. Celtic Christian communities which had the living of a rule as one of their basic elements in forming community are a model for the future of parish ministry.

For people to live a rule of life effectively the congregation must strive to be the kind of congregation I envision. The church must provide training for ministry, education, for faith development, good vital worship and prayer, and opportunities for mission and ministry, the work of the church. The congregation must strive to be a community.

Chapter Four

Creating Community

We can see that Celtic Christian communities can provide a model for parish ministry today, that congregations need to be true communities and centers for prayer and spirituality, teaching, and ministry.

All of these ingredients must go together to create the recipe for community to meet the challenges of mission in the world of today. How do we bring about community? How do our churches become places where God is present, "thin spots" where God and humanity meet?

First, of all we have to realize that forming community is not easy. It is a continual process that, like the spiritual life, like the circle, is never finished; we are constantly becoming God's people, the Church. It can never happen without the grace of God, but it is the task of the Church to make it happen with God's assistance.

The most difficult part of becoming a community is giving up control. When everyone is included diversity can be uncomfortable and difficult. Human beings like to be with people like themselves. It is extremely difficult to live together when there are wide cultural differences in a congregation. Yet, our culture is becoming more diverse. In most urban areas there is no longer one race or cultural group that is the in majority. When people are realistic, another quality of community, they speak their minds and are honest. Problems and differences don't remain hidden for long; conflicts arise. The community has to resolve differences, listen and take all sides seriously, reach a decision, and abide by it. A community, by its very nature, is healing and converting so people become healthier in the process without some people being dominant over others. There is a spirit in the community and people can feel it, but in community the spirit is in control. For most people, who are used to having someone in charge and responsible, not being in control can be very uncomfortable; it is chaos.

The greatest challenge is for leadership. Instead of controlling everything, knowing everything that is going on in the congregation, clergy and lay leaders need to give up power. It means changing the whole model of leadership we are used to over to a new way of leadership, the way of God. It means enabling people to do ministry rather than just receive it. It means allowing them to plan and carry out activities and be responsible for their outcome. New leaders have to be recruited and their individual gifts discerned. The most difficult aspect is that when plans fail there is no one to blame. But when the community is successful everyone can celebrate.

The type of leadership it takes to guide a community is the most effective of all. It enables people to become leaders themselves. Clergy complain about the demands put on them to be people who meet everyone's need; in a community the responsibility of leadership is shared. Leadership must be "self-differentiated." A leader must be willing to make decisions and stand on them, doing what is best for the community.

While community is very difficult to attain, it is worth it. Most of us have never experienced real community and don't know how it feels. One of the best ways to bring it about is simply to have it be a vision of the parish. It should be part of a parish mission statement. Often mission statements are incredibly unrealistic; they say things about the parish that are not true or realized yet. It is acceptable to have such a mission as long as it is a vision of what a congregation wants to become. One purpose or mission of every parish is to become a true community, the church. Community should be a stated goal of the congregation.

Perhaps it would be beneficial to have the five aspects of community posted somewhere prominent to remind people in leadership of the goal. If you are going to attain community you must have the ideal ever before you. The church board of directors and people should have an understanding of what community is and why it is the Church. They should know the basis for a theology of community.

A further goal is to be a welcoming congregation. A critical part of being a community is to welcome and include all people. Hospitality is crucial. The main time welcoming occurs is on Sunday mornings or at events that include many people outside the church, like weddings and funerals. A community must have a welcoming program and a method of including people once they become part of the congregation.

All of these ways of attaining community were part of the Celtic model of ministry in community. John Finney points this out in his book *Recovering the Past: Celtic and Roman Mission*.[1] I believe the Celtic communities always had this ideal before them. In their understanding of the circle enclosing their community they had a visible sign of the mission of the community to try and make their community a place where the veil between God and earth was lifted. Everyone was welcome. There was a rule of hospitality. A chief ministry was a monk whose job it was to welcome all newcomers, introduce them to everyone and find them a place to stay. The monk would then introduce the person to the abbot who would ask what the person was seeking so the community could provide for their needs. By doing this the Celtic Christians said they might "welcome an angel unawares."

As Finney points out the model of the Roman Church was different. The Romans considered everyone who was not a Roman as uncivilized. In fact, the word "barbarian" was coined from the sound Celts and other non-Romans made when they spoke in their native tongue, which sounded like "ba, ba" to the Roman ear. The Romans believed the Christian message

---

[1] John Finney, *Recovering the Past: Celtic and Roman Mission* (London: Darton, Longman and Todd, 1996).

could only be received when the person was "civilized" enough. As George G. Hunter puts it, "bluntly stated, the Roman model for reaching people (who are 'civilized' enough) is: (1) Present the Christian message; (2) Invite them to decide to believe in Christ and become Christians; and (3) If they decide positively, welcome them into the church and its fellowship."[2] This is the current model of evangelism in the Church.

The Celtic model for receiving people into the community was "(1) You first establish community with people, or bring them into the fellowship of your community of faith. (2) Within fellowship, you engage in conversation, ministry, prayer, and worship. (3) In time, as they discover that they now believe, you invite them to commit."[3] People need to belong before they believe. Most people who join churches must feel welcome before they will become part of things.

The Celtic people, as we have discussed before, were very tolerant of religious diversity; all religion was part of the search for God. They incorporated much of their earlier beliefs into the Church. In a sense there were no pagans or barbarians, those who were outside of the church community. All people were searching for God. All people were part of the new family, the new clan of Christians.

To bring people into the Church today we have to assume the same. All people are looking for God and community. No one person is better than another. The members of the church often spend a great deal of time and energy talking about how barbarian those outside the church are, especially those of other religions. Why do we assume there was no spirituality before Christianity or there is none in other cultures? To belittle a person because of their lack of faith, as we perceive it, is insulting. If anything, it will drive an individualist who must find out the meaning of life for themselves away.

People are looking for these basic things, believing and belonging. They are not interested in what they perceive the

---

[2] George G. Hunter III, *The Celtic Way of Evangelism: How Christianity Can Reach the West . . . Again* (Nashville: Abingdon Press, 2000) 53.
   [3] Ibid.

Church is doing much of the time—arguing about theological and moral issues that have little to do with real life. Western society and churches have forgotten about the "middle things of life" since the Enlightenment, Hunter points out. Life is explained and lived at three levels. One level is the factors in life our senses can apprehend. At this level we plow a field, plant a crop, fix a car, do practical tasks. Another level is beyond the level of our senses; these are the ultimate questions of the universe. These are the questions most theologians deal with today. People are actually interested in the things in the middle of these two levels.

These are the "questions of uncertainty of the near future, the crises of present life, and the unknowns of the past."[4] People are interested in the ordinary things of life and how God is involved, particularly in times when things do not go as planned or hoped. The Celtic communities meet these needs first. People must leave the church each Sunday with the resources to face the issues of real life. A community is realistic.

A community must be a place where people can deal with realistic life issues. A task of the people in community is to show they are really concerned with these issues. Likewise, they live in a special way that answers these questions and they show it. Dominic Crossan describes the kingdom of God just this way, "a community of radical and unbroken equality in which individuals are in direct contact with each other and with God."[5] The goal of the kingdom, what God ultimately wants in the world, is the goal of community. The Christian community, in dealing realistically with life is a place where God and humanity meet.

A Christianity community today must have programs that meet these middle issues. It must be a center for spirituality where people are taught to pray to deal with life spiritually, a center for education teaching on life's issues, such as parenting or dealing with elderly parents, and center for doing mission and ministry. Most of all, it must be a welcoming community.

[4] Ibid., 30–31.
[5] Andrew Harvey, *Son of Man: The Mystical Path to Christ* (New York: Jeremy Torder and Putnam, 1999) 22–23.

The Church today must meet the people where they are; we must understand their culture. In most of the Church we do not do this; the Church is out of touch. The majority of people in the Western world no longer listen to organ music or love evensong. They speak a different language than the words in the prayer book. Yet we insist on these forms of worship. The problem is, we do all of these things for the people already in the Church, ourselves. How do we attract new people yet minister to the people who like it the way it is? Arlin Rothauge has taught us about "parallel development." You must minister to those who like one form of worship, for instance, and those who prefer a more contemporary version at the same time. The programs run parallel to each other.[6] What we need is a service to attract people outside of the Church culture and one for those within.

The Celtic Christians did this. They sent out teams of people who went to the people. They lived with the people, made friends with them, and made them belong. The people who already had made a commitment lived in the enclosed communities. The people who lived in the center or *termon* with the presence of the saint were the holy people who were trained as evangelists or lived a more devout rule.

We need two types of churches today within the community: those who go to the people and those who minister to the people at home. All the time the two are blended with each other. Many evangelical churches do this already with "seeker" services on Sundays and regular worship during the week.

Everything the Celtic Christians did was in this two-tiered fashion. To do this we must put as one of our first priorities bringing people to faith through belonging. A whole part of our programs must be to do just that. Most churches today spend most of their energy on themselves, ministering to members, administration, and debating issues. Little, if any time is devoted to going to people outside the congregation with the

---

[6] Arlin Rothauge, *Parallel Development: A Pathway for Exploring Change and a New Future in Congregational Life* (Congregational Center Development Services, New York, Episcopal Church).

message of Christ or helping them to belong to the community and then believe.

One way to establish community is to enable people to live a rule of life. When people in the Celtic world were ready for a larger commitment to the church after baptism they took a rule of life. The living of a rule of life assists and supports the manifestation of authentic community. It serves as a guide for people and the parish as a whole to evaluate how well we are living as a real community. Having a rule of life enables people to see themselves as being different, being able to pray, grow, and work in the world in ways that make a difference, because they are done with God. It is living a rule in the parish that that has an effect on people's lives and shows again the importance of belonging in community.

A rule of life is simply a guide for living the Christian life. It contains the measure by which people conduct the practice of their religion and also by which they evaluate how well they are doing. When people joined with a Celtic Christian community they gave up their families and clans and their status in the secular world. Automatically their life was reordered.[7] The new Christian community became the person's family.[8]

Each community had a rule but it seems that each had a different one.[9] Some were lenient and others were very strict. Some extended only to the celibate monks or nuns but others set the behavior for all people living or associating with the community. The Rule of Mochuda, for example extended to lay communities beyond the community enclosure by setting guidelines for kings as well as those who worked for the community and their dependents.[10] When people followed a rule like this they were given a semi-religious status and regarded as part of the monastic family.[11] Both sexes were included. Some monastic communities such as Kildare had both men

---

[7] Bitel, *Isle of the Saints,* 88.
[8] Ibid., 89.
[9] Ibid., 136.
[10] Ibid.
[11] Ibid., 124.

and women living in the celibate community.[12] Everyone who lived or associated with a Christian community had to change their lifestyle from the secular world. They wanted to be different.[13] All of them were considered to be "monks," even if they lived within normal family life.[14] This model for living a rule can be carried over to parish life today.

For people to live a rule of life effectively the congregation must strive to be a community. The church community must provide training for ministry, education, faith development, good vital worship and prayer, and opportunity for mission and ministry.

The rule of life is a central part of a Christian community. When people join a parish as a baptized member or are confirmed or received they should be urged to take a rule as their guide to living out their baptismal covenant. Not everyone will take a rule. Those who observe a rule can keep their rule to themselves or share it with others. There should be no special ceremony or liturgy when they commit to a rule. Everyone could renew or begin their rule on the Sunday of the Baptism of Christ in January. In this way they begin living a rule of life as a New Year's resolution. Also, it is a reminder that the rule is a way to follow your baptismal covenant; it does not make you more special than anyone else, every Christian in today's world is different than the dominant culture.

The rule should be simple and flexible. People can live in a very rigorous way or a lenient one depending on their ability. People should be urged to take a rule that is challenging yet feasible to do. It must be flexible enough to fit into today's fast pace and complexity of life.

A suggested rule of life is the basic monastic rule that is present in all of the great world religions. The rule is a threefold intent.[15] What will a person do to:

[12] Sheldrake, *Living Between Worlds,* 42.
[13] Bitel, *Isle of the Saints,* 142.
[14] Sheldrake, *Living Between Worlds,* 36.
[15] Based upon the Caim Community Rule, The House of Prayer, P.O. Box 5888, Collegeville, Minnesota 56321, U.S.A.

Be a person of prayer . . . ?
Be committed to spiritual
   growth and transformation . . . ?
Be compassionate in our
   actions and relationships . . . ?

What will the person do to be a person of prayer and to grow and be transformed into the person God created them to be? What is the action or ministry as a result? This is the basic rule of work, study, and prayer. It is flexible for a wide range of commitment and ability. People should be advised to write down their rule each year, but many prefer to keep it in confidence with God. Do not publish who is living a rule so people will not feel or be perceived by others as especially committed or holy. A great failing of other renewal movements in the Church is that they often have created divisions in the Church or cliques which exclude others. It is difficult to know who is living a rule, but people should be encouraged to share their rule with clergy or with others who are living a rule of life to see how it is going.

The rule of life is a mutual idea of the Rev. Dr. David Keller, the past director of the House of Prayer in Collegeville, Minnesota, and myself. Dr. Keller first proposed the idea in 1993 in a paper, *The Caim Community: Offering a Monastic Rule of Life for Men and Women Whose Monastery is the Family, the Workplace and Daily Life in a Complex World.*[16]

Living a rule of life creates a community. In living a rule people feel like they are different than others because they live a spiritual life. They are reminded, however, that they are not superior because of it. A sign of God's grace is humility. A rule of life is a guide for them on the spiritual journey. It gives them a process for renewal and evaluation of their spiritual life. Living a rule of life helps people see that prayer, study, and growth and ministry make a difference in their lives and

---

[16] David Keller, *The Caim Community: Offering a Monastic Rule of Life for Men and Women Whose Monastery is the Family, the Workplace and Daily Life in a Complex World* (The House of Prayer, P.O. Box 5888, Collegeville, Minnesota 56321, 1993).

the lives of others. People are enabled to vision their transformation, as they become the Body of Christ in the world.

The community becomes the same as the Celtic communities. It is a place encircled by God in the *Caim,* the sacred circle. Because of the Celtic vision of community we call those who live in community with the basic threefold rule, the *Caim* Community. The foundation of the parish striving to be a community is the rule of life. Mainly, it makes God real in people's daily lives, at home, the workplace, and the congregation.

In my doctoral thesis I researched how effective a rule of life was in people's lives.[17] There was conclusive evidence that it made the Christian life more effective and meaningful to people. They could feel God in their lives and see God in the world. They could feel the presence of God in the community of which they were part. The parish became a vibrant place for prayer and spiritual development, learning, and growth and ministry to the larger community. Stewardship and giving increased. The church continues to attract more people and to grow in numbers. The Vestry has "building community" as a stated goal in the parish mission statement. By doing all of the things above a community has formed. In being a true community the parish church can meet the greatest challenge of our society—individualism and the isolation of people.

What is the theology of community? The Celtic people had a concept of community inherent in their clan system. Christianity easily fit into their worldview. Their special form of evangelism also was formed around their culture and how they related to others, their "habits of the heart." The Celtic people were not perfect, in fact their society was very violent; the clans didn't love each other but competed for land usually with violence as a result. They raided each other's farms for cattle or slaves. They collected severed heads as trophies and displayed them on their belts, the tack of their horses or chariots, and their houses. There is evidence that the Celts com-

---

[17] Jerry C. Doherty, *The Caim Community: Early Celtic Christian Communities as a Model in Parish Ministry* (The Seabury Institute, Seabury-Western Theological Seminary, 1998).

mitted human sacrifice. Yet, in just about two hundred years Ireland, for example, went from a society of non-Christians to the Age of Saints.

Besides the culture of community among the Celts the Celtic Christians got much of their theology from the early Church in the Mideast, especially the Desert Fathers and the teachers of the East. The Celts read *The Life of St. Anthony* by Athanasius.[18] They traveled to North Africa and learned about the forms of monasticism and the ascetical life of hermits in the desert. They took these models for monasticism back to Celtic lands.

They radically adopted the idea of the monastery at home in Celtic areas. John Cassian visited the desert and saw the saints there himself and described what he saw in his *Institutes*. He interviewed the great abbots, hermits, and teachers and recorded what they said in his *Conferences*. He took these back to Gaul and formed his own community. St. Martin of Tours formed a community after the Desert Fathers. The Celtic people were in constant dialogue with the East. It was a time when Christianity was in the early stages of developing a theology in relation to the culture it was trying to reach. Because the Eastern monastic movement was in reaction to a culture that was Christian in name only the early monks had much to say about society. They had fled to the desert to escape temptations that were there especially now that Christianity was not counterculture. It was legal with the Edict of Milan, declared part of the state and now part of culture. The culture had adapted to Christianity and the faith to the culture. The monks felt it had adapted too much; they could only live a true Christian life away from society. The Celts took all of these ideas and theology as their own. They collected the works of the Church Fathers for their monastic libraries. The library at Iona for instance contained many works by the Latin Fathers.[19]

Today the Orthodox Church still sees the Celtic Christians as an unbroken link with the East. There are icons of the saints

[18] Hunter, *The Celtic Way of Evangelism,* 27.

[19] Thomas O'Loughlin, *Celtic Theology: Humanity, World and God in Early Celtic Writings* (London: Continuum, 2000) 81.

of Ireland, Scotland, and Wales. We can see the evidence on the high crosses in Ireland and Wales such as the cross at Pen Mon on Angelsey which has a panel depicting Anthony's temptation in the desert.[20] We can even see the evidence in the great heresy of the age, Pelagianism. After all Pelagius was a Celt who had traveled and lived in the great theological centers of the East. The combination with Eastern theology and the Celtic West is definitely seen in the writing of the ninth-century Irish theologian John Scotus Eriugena. The Christians of the Celtic world definitely had a relationship with the Eastern Church.

Theological reflection on the understanding of God in community is very thought provoking. The idea of the presence of the Creator in community is biblical. Paul Hanson's work *A People Called: The Growth of Community in the Bible,* traces the theme throughout the biblical story.[21] The community is formed when the people flee from Egypt at the Passover and are rescued by God from pharaoh's army at the Red Sea. As they enter the Promised Land the Law is designed to protect the poor and helpless so the people of God will never become the oppressor but the community will be preserved. The theme of community continues in the biblical story.

God is in the community of human beings by God's very nature. The Celtic Christians were very trinitarian. They rarely talked about the persons of the Trinity, Father, Son, and Holy Spirit separately, but as one God, the Trinity. The Trinity is the God of community. God is always with the community of the people of God throughout the Bible. Elizabeth Johnson says, "divine trinity must be seen to consist not in the identity of an absolute subject but in the living *koinea,* the community, among three distinct persons."[22] Because God is Trinity, three distinct Persons in one, God is community.

[20] John Sharkey, *Celtic High Crosses of Wales* (Llanrwst, Wales: Gwasg Carreg Gwalch, 1998) 104.

[21] Paul Hanson, *The People Called: The Growth of Community in the Bible* (San Francisco: Harper and Row, 1986).

[22] Elizabeth Johnson, *She Who Is: The Mystery of God in Feminist Discourse* (New York: Crossroad Publishing Company, 1992) 207.

The early Church Fathers would agree; the Church is the Body of Christ; it is the place where human beings, and the whole creation are transfigured into God. This was brought about by the grace of God in Christ. When God emptied God's self to become a human being Christ came into the world. It was in Christ's emptying on the cross that he became truly the link to human beings. The early Fathers called this giving or emptying of oneself *kenosis*. The emptying of oneself in Christ begins the process of *theosis* or deification.

Deification is how God works in us by the grace of the Holy Spirit to make us into the person God created us to be. We can see at a glance that this is what the Celtic people believed spiritually; by the grace of God in Christ you can become one with God. It was the basis of all their spiritual exercises which were patterned after those in the East.

It is in the Church, the community, that *theosis* most occurs. When people who have given themselves to God in Christ come together they are in the process of deification; they all come together as one. It is in the Church that they are reborn.

This theology was most expressed by Maximus the Confessor who lived in Constantinople and North Africa 580 C.E. to 662 C.E. at the same time as the Age of Saints was occurring in the Celtic world. Maximus built on much of the theology of the early Church, especially Evagrius of Pontus (d. 399 C.E.), the mysterious fifth-century personality, Dionysius the Areopagite, and the Cappadocians, Basil of Caesarea and his brother Gregory of Nyssa, and Gregory of Nazianzen, who lived in the fourth century.[23]

The Church is the visible aspect of God in the world. When the people of God join as one they join with Christ as one and are the presence of Christ. The Church therefore is made up of individual bodies joining into one Body of Christ. All that the Church does in community are the "material signs of the spiritual world."[24] The Church began with the first people in the

---

[23] Jaroslav Pelican (Introduction), *Maximus the Confessor: Selected Writings,* trans. George C. Berthold (London: SPCK, 1985) 6.

[24] Vladimir Loosky, *The Mystical Theology of the Eastern Church* (London: James Clark and Company Ltd., 1957) 189.

mystical foundation of the world. When the first human beings searched for the divine, the Church was formed.[25] The Church could include any group that comes together searching for spiritual meaning, but it occurs most in the Church.

The Church does this transformation in the sacraments, the signs of God's presence and action in community, the Church. The first sacrament is the Scriptures when they are read in church. The second is baptism, the sign that God has begun the deification of the person. The third is the Eucharist, the celebration and great thanksgiving for the life, death, and resurrection of Christ in the bread and wine, the Body and Blood of Christ. "The Eucharist transforms the faithful into itself," Maximus said. We become part of Christ and Christ part of us. Gregory of Nyssa wrote, "eat and drink deeply, intoxicated in Christ himself."[26]

Maximus the Confessor said that when the Church comes together in faith an energy starts to be created. This energy, he said, begins deification of the Church and the people in it. The process of this energy transforming people in community he called *perichoresis. Perichoresis* meant "rotation" or "completion of a cycle." Literally it means "circle dance." Maximus said there is a double movement: human to divine and divine to human. In the movement of the divine toward human God becomes accessible to human nature in Jesus Christ. Human beings become part of God, *theosis,* in the process of rotation, *perichoresis.* There is a real human movement toward God; human beings enter and affect God and God enters people and transforms them.

Maximus believed this movement was mutual and not one-sided, but there is an order to the movement. God moves toward the human first. God wants to have a relationship with each person. The person needs to respond to the offer of relationship to the Divine. But once relationship begins *perichoresis,* the movement or rotation to God starts and continues. The energy of God is humanized and human energy is made divine.

[25] Ibid., 111.
[26] Oliver Clément, *The Roots of Christian Mysticism* (Hyde Park, New York: The New City Press, 1995) 111.

The energy of *perichoresis* particularly is produced in a community of human beings who are all part of this rotating relationship with God. They come together, like atoms rubbing together, creating a nuclear reaction; they produce energy, the energy of the Spirit. God's energy in *perichoresis* can also be described as light hitting a person. God's power in community is like sun on your back. You feel the energy and it warms you.

To me an example of this is the experience of Pentecost in the New Testament when the disciples attracted many people by speaking in different languages (Acts 1:1-13). People from all over the ancient world at the time were in Jerusalem for the festival. They spoke many different tongues but when they heard the disciples praising God they all heard them in their own language. They understood and in the understanding a relationship began with the disciples and God in Christ. In a sense community was formed. *Perichoresis,* the rotation of God to humankind, and God to humanity, had begun. The people felt the energy like "tongues of fire" as the disciples spoke. It was like air filling a vacuum. People felt the Spirit. Pentecost, I believe, is an example of *perichoresis,* the energy of God and the presence of God in community.

With this power I believe the Church can do anything. The Great Exchange of God with humanity and humanity to God starts when people begin relationship with God individually and then come together in community. The Church community itself is a sacrament, an outward and visible sign of the presence of God. The Church is in the process of changing all of creation to be the Church.

The transfiguration of the world to God begins in God's community the center in the circle of *perichoresis.* Maximus the Confessor says that the Holy Spirit is present in all people, without exception as the preserver of all things, but he is particularly present to those bearing the witness of Jesus Christ. God makes children of all of them. Yet another group he deifies. "Thus in relation to union with God, the universe is arranged in concentric circles about a center which is occupied by the church, the members of which become children of God." There is a yet smaller, narrower circle of those "who have understanding who enter into union with God."[27] Sound familiar? It is if Maximus the Confessor is describing a Celtic Christian community with its concentric rings and its center of the saints.

The work of the Church is to constantly live and celebrate *perichoresis* and be an example. The early Celtic Christians did this task. An example is how they gave thanks and celebrated the eucharistic prayer, the Great Thanksgiving. They celebrated the Eucharist as if it was "an encounter crossing several thresholds."[28]

It gave thanks that earth was part of heaven, especially in this place of celebration. It strains toward the end when all will be as God intends; it recalls the kingdom. It remembers the saints and joins them. It recalls that we are free in Christ; all people are accepted and wanted. It recalls our worshiping activity and ministry, but more truly the ministry of Christ, that occurs among us when we live in him. The Celts celebrated all of this. They used a loaf of bread so people could eat a large piece. They produced huge chalices that would hold over two large bottles of wine so people could not just sip, but drink fully of the wine. The chalice often had handles on either side to aid in the drinking.[29] Often clergy concelebrated to show that no one was dominant. The Eucharist was a feast celebrating and giving thanks for what God is doing in the world.

This attitude disappeared in the West in the eleventh through the thirteenth centuries. It was replaced by a notion that liturgy supplies what is needed to gain sanctifying grace and ultimately salvation. A person went to church and received Communion to be "saved" to be served by an elite priesthood. Previously in the East the people joined the epiclesis by their amens[30] and the bread and wine were given to the people to be taken home and given out by the leader of the household.[31] The community really understood what God does in community.

[27] Loosky, *The Mystical Theology of the Eastern Church*, 178.
[28] O'Loughlin, *Celtic Theology*, 128.
[29] Ibid., 135.
[30] Clément, *The Roots of Christian Mysticism*, 112.
[31] Ibid., 123.

The genius of the Celtic Christians is that they knew God as present in true community. They knew God gave new life to communities who served as centers to promote community among people. Because of the place of God in community they modeled their own congregations as centers to enable people to grow in relationship to God, individually and in association with others. They believed that when they lived this way God really was present inside the circle that surrounded their home representing the great circle of life that enveloped them and the universe and brought new life.

I believe that the Christians of Celtic lands have shown us a way to follow. I believe people are irresistibly attracted to community because community is where God is most evident and people need God in their lives. God is in the Church and its congregations. We stand on holy ground.

Chapter Five

A Crisis of Faith

Another crisis of our time is a crisis of faith. Many people today simply do not believe in the presence of God in the world or in their lives. If God exists at all God is very silent.

This way of thinking is due to many factors. One cause is the Enlightenment which emerged out of the Renaissance in Europe. The Enlightenment taught the power of humanity and the human mind. The philosopher Rene Descartes said "I think, therefore I am." This differed with the thought of the early Christian theology; a medieval version of the same thought, which included the Celts, might have been, "I think, therefore God is." The new idea, coupled with the work of scientists like Sir Isaac Newton, who proposed the law of gravity, saw the universe as governed by unseen forces. Human beings were beginning to discover that there might be other powers besides God. Building on the work of David Hume, Immanuel Kant refuted the existence of God. Kant said human beings had created God in their minds. Actually, most of the philosophers of the time were really Deists; they believed God existed but was far off; God created the earth and kept everything running like a watchmaker, but then had withdrawn into heaven altogether and had not intervened in human life since. Deism was as far as they were willing to go; A. N. Wilson in his book *God's Funeral,* that traces the whole intellectual movement of disbelief in God, writes:

> Safer to say you are a Deist, and not rock the boat. The Deist position kept God happily in His place. So long as He was far away, there was no need to kill Him off, this mechanical Deity. Besides like President Coolidge in Dorothy Parker's famous quip, it would have been difficult to know whether the Deist God were dead or alive.[1]

God had abandoned the world to run on its own. The next step was obviously to do away with God altogether. At the same time these philosophers were writing, the people around the Western world were getting rid of their kings appointed by divine right, such as in France and America. As we have mentioned before, the founders of the United States were primarily Deists and products of the Enlightenment.

Science continued to prove that things in the universe ran on their own; we began to understand more of the pattern of the universe and with understanding came more questioning of God. Charles Darwin proposed his theory of evolution which was not compatible with the biblical story of creation. The Scriptures themselves were scrutinized by scholars and the whole historicity of the Bible debated. Histories of the Church were written that exposed the scandals of the popes and superstitions of the medieval Church. Some scholars even doubted the historical person of Jesus and questioned his miracles, especially the Resurrection. Sigmund Freud explored the human mind and how it further created its own reality.

Most of the people had never read all of these authors but their ideas became part of their thinking. Mainly, people were not experiencing God. God was just no longer relevant. The First World War and then the Second World War made people further question their belief in God. What kind of God would allow so many people to die? How could God permit the Holocaust to take place? The Church is powerless; it didn't do anything to prevent war or genocide; in the case of the death of millions of Jews it even supported their demise by centuries of anti-Semitism. Where is God? God must be dead.

[1] A. N. Wilson, *God's Funeral* (London: John Murray, 1999) 29.

For most people God and the Church are not part of their lives anymore. The belief that God is dead has intensified in our culture, a new "habit of the heart." Coupled with individualism people see no need to be part of a corporate body of faith. The Church and belief in God make no difference.

The Reformation of the Church itself, as part of the Renaissance, taught people they can do things for themselves. Human thinking and creativity is awesome in its effectiveness. The Reformers as a result taught people they should "have faith" for themselves to "be saved" by the theistic God of the Universe. Just faith that's all! You either have it or you don't. If you don't (and most of us don't have faith off and on), you are doomed. There is nothing to believe in besides making life as comfortable as possible for you and your family and friends. It's just fine to be among the comfortable of the Western world, the "haves and have yachts," while forgetting the rest of the planet. There is a tendency to expect nothing of much depth in life, or nihilism, expecting nothing at all. At least people ask, "is this all there is?"

In Bishop John Spong's recent book, *Why Christianity Must Change or Die: A Bishop Speaks to Believers in Exile,* he says what we all know; people may believe in God but if they believe at all they don't believe in a God that is out of the world who intervenes when God feels like it. Spong feels there are millions of believers in exile from the churches because of this belief. The Church perpetuates the myth of the theistic God in many ways. The most vivid example, Spong writes, are the creeds, the statements of faith used in the churches:

> The words of the Apostle's Creed, and its later expansion known as the Nicene Creed, were fashioned inside a worldview that no longer exists. . . . If the God I worship must be identified with these ancient creedal words in any literal sense, God would become for me not just unbelievable but in fact no longer worthy of being a subject of my devotion.[2]

[2] John Shelby Spong, *Why Christianity Must Change or Die: A Bishop Speaks to Believers in Exile: A New Reformation of the Church's Faith and Practice* (San Francisco: Harper Collins, 1998) 4.

Bishop Spong says these types of statements and language and concepts which perpetuate the belief in a theistic God must change. The future of the Church rests on refashioning these symbols by which Christianity is understood. Creedal patterns would have to be rethought in the light of contemporary understanding of the world. The job of the Church is to reinvite these believers in exile back to the faith and "into the mystery of God."[3]

Polls in the United States may indicate that Spong is right. Most people in the country say they believe in God but only a smaller portion belong to a community of faith or worship in a church regularly. When asked why they believe but don't go to church the response is summarized by "because the church makes no difference" and "the people there are no different than me."

The churches respond to the crisis of belief mostly by defending their own belief. "We still believe" they say. The faith inside the churches may be fine but outside of the institution, the fact is, there is a change in belief and it is not in the Church.

But, people need to believe. In fact, that is the purpose of being human. The meaning of life is to be in relationship to God. This is what makes us human because unlike other creatures we know we are going to die. To deny or simply forget about God makes us like spiritual sleep walkers in life. Our very need for God is a source of grace because God is drawn to our yearning for meaning and belief.

If the churches want people to return and believe the churches must be relevant to life. They must be a community of faith and teach people to believe. What is needed is a new mysticism. Mysticism simply means to feel acutely the presence of God. A person who is a mystic is someone who knows God exists because they feel it. God is not far away, a theistic God, but a God that is close by. The meaning of the coming of Christ is to reveal what God has already done. In being a human being, in entering into time Christ has shown that God has made us

---

[3] Ibid., 19–21.

part of God; God is on earth and we are in heaven. God is not just close; God is in our hearts, the place where we believe.

People don't just need to believe; they need to feel it. Marcus Borg, who, as a New Testament scholar looking for a historical Jesus, has often been accused of destroying people's faith, has this to say about true believing.

> I want . . . (to talk) about a very familiar Christian phrase—believing in Jesus—and how it is related to the image of Christian life that has emerged. . . . For those who grew up in the church, believing in Jesus was important. For me what that phrase used to mean, in my childhood and early adulthood, was "believing things about Jesus." To believe in Jesus meant to believe what the Gospels and the church said about Jesus. That was easy when I was a child, and became more and more difficult as I grew older.
>
> But I now see that believing in Jesus can (and does) mean something different from that. The change is pointed to by the root meaning of the word *believe*. *Believe* did not originally mean believing a set of doctrines or teachings; in Greek and Latin its roots mean "to give one's heart to." The heart is the self at its deepest level. *Believing*, therefore, does not consist of giving one's mental assent to something, but involves a much deeper level of one's self. Believing in Jesus does not mean believing doctrines about him. Rather it means to give one's heart at its deepest level.[4]

Believing in this way is the moving from secondhand religion to firsthand religion, from believing what you have heard or been taught about Jesus to being in relationship with Jesus. This type of believing makes God and Christ alive, here and now. Believing with the heart in relationship makes you a mystic. *In believing this way you can experience God firsthand.*

---

[4] Marcus Borg, *Meeting Jesus Again for the First Time: The Historical Jesus and the Heart of Contemporary Faith* (San Francisco: Harper Collins, 1995) 137.

The Church has discouraged this way of deeper believing because it is risky revolutionary business. If you have large groups of people in a deep relationship with God then they might come up with new schemes of living the faith in a real way. How would you sort out all the crazy people from the sane? What if something is proposed that threatens the power of religious authority? The Church hierarchy would lose control. Everything would be chaos. Almost all of the mystics who wrote or were vocal about their beliefs have been questioned, persecuted, or silenced by the Church. Chaos, as we have discussed before, can be a sign of true community, people giving up control and trusting in God.

It is believing in the heart about God that is the faith people are looking for. For us to be content, creative, compassionate, and fully human we must have this kind of faith. Indeed, the survival of humanity and the planet may depend upon it. We need the kind of knowledge and wisdom that we can only get from God to solve the problems of our time. There is no other answer or power strong enough to face the new challenges of our earth, poverty, overpopulation, violence, prejudice, environmental disaster, and disbelief and hopelessness. It has to be the role of the Church to live and teach the deep belief and faith of mysticism.

It is from imagination that the mystical journey begins. Imagination is the use of the mind and body to create symbols. Symbols enlighten us to see life in new ways, to be aware of the presence of God in the ordinary things of life. Symbols especially allow us to have a vision of the future and a hope for better times to come.

The creative use of imagination is lacking in our culture. We predominately think in a different way; we use our left brain more than our right brain. Psychologists have determined that the cerebrum has two "hemispheres," the right and left sides of the brain.

The left hemisphere controls the right side of the body and mental functions, while the right hemisphere controls the left side of the body and the perception of spatial relationships. Left brain cultures are filled with people that are very rational, scientific while right-brained cultures are artistic, emotional, and imaginative.[5] Our Western culture today is definitely left-brained. This is the problem we have in thinking in imaginative ways. We have to have imagination to believe in God in a deep firsthand way. We are not developed in an imaginative way. We don't value the arts like a right-brained culture. We even feel that when we "imagine" something it is not real. In a right-brained culture imagination is real and who is to say it is not?

"Christianity is in the first place an Oriental religion, and it is a mystical religion. These assertions sound strange today, in an age when it is generally assumed that to be a Christian means to live a good life," writes Jean-Claude Barreau.[6] Christianity is a mystical religion, a religion that pivots on deep firsthand belief that only comes with imagination. It is based on experience and feeling rather than knowledge or rational thinking. This is not to say that knowledge is unimportant but mystical faith cannot be built on it. Christianity comes from an Oriental culture from the Mideast; it comes from an imaginative right-brained world. Ever since Augustine of Hippo the West attempted to rationalize Christianity and codify it into a set of beliefs. Augustine was a mystic but in his rationalization of Christianity with knowledge he set a direction of thinking in motion that lasts to this day. Orthodoxy, "right belief" became more important than orthopraxis, "right practice."[7]

The Celtic culture was Oriental and it was imaginative and creative. The people we call the Celts came from the Mideast and expanded westward across Europe and after being conquered and absorbed by Rome, their culture that remained became the "Celtic fringe" we know today. They were a people who told imaginative mythical stories. The stories were so sacred and the spoken word so divine they were all memorized, not written. The bards or poets were one of the most powerful groups having a spiritual vocation as well as an artistic one; it is often only in verse that you can express knowledge of God.

[5] Hunter, *The Celtic Way of Evangelism*, 71.

[6] Clément, *The Roots of Christian Mysticism;* Jean-Claude Barreau, preface, 7.

[7] Finney, *Recovering the Past,* 119.

Celtic artists created beautiful jewelry, colorful textiles, and in Christian times ornate decorated manuscripts like the famous Book of Kells. They wrote fantastic stories of the lives of the saints filled with stupendous miracles. The Celtic people were accomplished musicians and employed music in their worship. They were people of great imagination.

Once again, they shared the imagination and mysticism of the Oriental Church from the desert and Byzantium of the third to the seventh centuries. They were part of the Wisdom of the Desert and the teaching of the Church Fathers. Their Church was a mystical Church. It was a Church of faith first-hand. Each facet of life was intensely spiritual. Prayer and meditation were constant, thus the beautiful prayers collected by Alexander Carmichael in the Highlands and islands of western Scotland, for every purpose from plowing the field to lighting the fire. The Church was monastic; people lived the faith and were taught a life of prayer living side by side the monks.

The Celtic churches or communities were mystical Christianity. They knew God firsthand. If we strive to recover a real personal spiritual relationship with God we can learn from them. We can find many answers to the problems we face in the world and the life of the Church.

In teaching people the spiritual life, the Celtic Christians, first of all, saw the spiritual life as a spiritual journey. The relationship with God has no beginning or end; it is always at the beginning. The early Church Fathers shared this belief; to be a human being is always to be searching for God even though God is always there. We are not content until we are part of God, until we are in union with God. It is being one with God that is the spiritual goal of life. Reaching the goal is an ongoing process. We get glimpses and insights into God. Each time we reach a new awareness of God we want more and are given a vacuum in the heart that will not rest until it is filled again. The spiritual journey is vividly symbolized in the cross slabs of the tenth century found at Clonmacnois in Ireland. The crosses are covered with a Celtic key pattern, a maze within the cross, symbolizing the spiritual twists and turns of life. They all lead to a circle in the center of the cross, the "motionless-mover" where God dwells. It is at the center of the cross where God and human beings meet.[8]

The understanding of life as a spiritual journey appeals to many people today. People in our time are searching but never find the answers. The largest section in many bookstores is the self-help section. In their individualism people must find out the meaning of life for themselves. They want to find out one truth or system that will meet all their needs. To find out that the truth is there are no perfect answers is a revelation of freedom to seekers of God. Even though many people search for one answer they still are put off by religious fundamentalists who are intolerant of those outside their belief system. In fact, many people see mainline Christianity in the same way, a group of hypocrites telling everyone else how to live. Christians must admit they don't know all the answers. We are then accused of "riding the fence," not having an opinion on anything. It is not true; we have a position; it is the middle. In ancient times the middle was the truth. Even when there was a paradox, truth was most present. When two truths seem to cancel one another out you have a paradox. It is at the middle of a paradox that we find the most truth. Actually most of life is a paradox; we are all people of paradox. We know the paradox of child and adult, male and female, heart and head, body and soul. The whole of the Gospel is the ultimate contradiction; God becomes a man; Jesus brings life from death. When you recognize paradox new ways of thinking emerge. Paradox was truth to the early theologians of the Church.[9] The Celts viewed the belief in paradox as part of the spiritual circle of life. Much of the spiritual life is contradiction, solitary and community, prayer and action; the Celtic Christians lived with the truth and contradiction of paradox.

As we have seen the Celtic people took the idea of the spiritual journey literally, going on journeys with no destination

---

[8] Derek Bryce, *Symbolism of the Celtic Cross* (York Beach, Maine: Samuel Weiser, Inc., 1995) 82–85.

[9] See Esther de Waal, ch. 2, *Living with Contradiction: An Introduction to Benedictine Spirituality*.

in mind. They coined the word *peregrinatio* to describe this journey with no destination. It is a word and concept found nowhere else in Christendom.[10] *Peregrinatio* really describes the truth of the spiritual journey; we don't know the destination. We cannot judge others for the answers they have found; we can only speak for ourselves. Likewise, the idea of the interior spiritual journey with no destination or one correct answer frees us to see God always in new and different ways. It also provides faith and tolerance when we venture into new areas where the road ends and there is no map. In our changing world we often enter new country that is foreign to us.

The early Church Fathers discerned three main stages in the spiritual way:

1. Praxis, the practice of ascesis, "the battle" to follow God, to transform the vital energy that has gone astray or been blocked in idolatry, above all self-idolatry, to give birth to the virtues that guide us to God.

2. Contemplation.

3. Direct personal union with God.[11]

It is on these stages of the spiritual life that the Celtic Christians based their praxis of Christianity. The first way they began the journey was in imaginative prayer. They believed in unceasing prayer and said prayers continuously in the oratory of the community. They memorized the psalms and often recited them on long journeys as they walked. They spent long periods in silent meditation in their cell or as they worked. They came together as a community for daily prayers at regular intervals. They sat or kneeled with their arms extended for long hours in the "cross vigil." St. Kevin of Glendalough was said to have held his arms extended for so long a bird made a nest in his hand.

---

[10] Esther de Waal, *The Celtic Way of Prayer: The Recovery of the Religious Imagination* (London: Hodder and Stoughton, 1996) 9.

[11] Clément, *The Roots of Christian Mysticism,* 133.

Again this belief came from the desert monastic movement. The organization of Celtic monastics who observed the strictest rules was based on the desert communities. St. Macarius of Egypt (ca. 300–ca. 390 C.E.), for instance was one of the early teachers of pure prayer. Macarius believed the soul and the flesh were one and as such the whole body comes in touch with God in prayer. The whole human being, body and soul, is called to divine glory. The presence of God permeates the world. To Macarius prayer stimulates the seed sown in the "bath of regeneration."[12] He taught the first form of the "Jesus" prayer, to say repeatedly the name of Christ until it became a prayer of the heart as natural as breathing. To pray in this way gives full knowledge that Jesus is present within us.[13] "He who links himself with Christ is one with him" (1 Cor 6:17). The goal is to become a living prayer.

Life is then spent in contemplation *(hesychia)* and continual internal unceasing prayer to God. This way of prayer began the hesychast movement in the desert monasteries including those of the Celtic world. The contemplation of God was best done in solitude so all of the Celtic saints sought times of solitary contemplation. Cuthbert went to Inner Farne, a small island off shore from Lindisfarne. Kevin went to a cave near Glendalough and Seirol to his cell. Goven found his cleft in the rocks. The monks sought virtually inaccessible places like Skellig Michael, a rock jutting up from the ocean at the end of the world, in southwest Ireland.

The early monastics and Church Fathers believed that if you followed this life of contemplation and Christian living you would achieve deification, union with God. If you did not achieve union in this life as the great saints had done you would achieve it at death. Meanwhile you would experience glimpses of God and know the existence of God is true. You will believe in the heart in personal relationship with God in Christ. Could any of us ask more in this life than to be sure of the presence of God and know in our hearts it is true?

---

[12] John Meyendorff, *St. Gregory Palamas and Orthodox Spirituality* (St. Vladimir's Seminary Press, 1974) 24–27.

[13] Ibid., 38.

The Fathers called this process of growing into God *theosis;* it is like an individual *perichoresis.* It changes people into the person God created them to be; it is the constant journey. God, shares God's energy with us. *Theosis* is a free act of God. God's essence remains inaccessible; it is sharing the energy of God that is a grace, a gift of God to make us part of God.[14] According to Maximus the energies and essence of God are united in Christ. All people are attached to Christ in his humanity and to his divine essence in his divinity. The nature of humanity remains the same. In this way the inaccessible transcendent God makes divinity available to humanity. It is a paradox, the way the inaccessible God becomes available.[15]

It is this kind of prayer that needs to be taught and lived in our congregations. It is the way that people can experience the presence of God. Churches should have training in different types of prayer so people can choose the best form for their use. Decisions at church meetings should be made with prayer. Meetings should include a time of contemplation. A goal of unceasing prayer in the church building should be included in the parish mission. There should be a service of contemplation as a regular part of worship.

An oratory, a place set aside just for prayer, should be designated in every church building. It needs to be a place where quiet is observed. The church needs to enable people to be alone from time to time, even building a hermitage in a place aside, or sponsoring regular retreats. Our society needs to slow down and be quiet. The early Church theologians and the Celtic Christians were right; it is possible to find God in community mixed with solitude and contemplative prayer. The combination makes mystics, people who acutely feel the presence of God. This formula would make the church the most exciting place you could possibly be. If people feel a real presence of God in their life it makes the church *a sacred place where you can actually know God.*

A further place where there is a crisis of faith is belief in the Scriptures. In the early Church mystical tradition, the reading

[14] Ibid., 43.
[15] Ibid., 46.

of the Bible, especially in church, is a sacrament, a time when we experience God. Science and discoveries of biblical criticism question the historicity and truth of the Bible. People no longer believe in the virgin birth or the parting of the Red Sea or Jesus walking on the water. With the discovery of outer space and even space travel, heaven is obviously not above us anymore. The Bible and the Nicene Creed, as John Spong says, represent a worldview that is not true or relevant in our time. If you can't believe the Bible, you can't believe the God presented in it. Reading the Scriptures ceases to be a sacrament for people; it is no longer an outward and visible sign of the presence of God. In fact hearing the violence, sexism, racism, and judgment presented in the Bible does the opposite; it convinces us to not believe in "that God."

We don't believe in the God who judges and destroys; we believe in the God of compassion and creation. The Bible is the story of how the people called the Jews came to know the one God and themselves as the chosen people. It continues with the coming of Christ and no longer do we have to please a God who sits in heaven and punishes us when we are bad and intervenes on earth when *he* chooses. God is within us in Christ; Christ shows God's love for us (John 3:16). We are one with God in Christ (John 17:22-23). We show the same love for God in our relationships with people. This is what we believe.

The Bible is not meant to be read literally but we continue to do so. Christianity is divided over how we read the Bible. "Fundamentalists" criticize "liberal" Christians for not taking the Bible word for word and only giving credence to the parts they approve, like the Deist Thomas Jefferson, who selected his own version of the Bible by "cut and paste."

The liberals accuse the conservatives of being inflexible and judgmental. Actually both sides read the Bible as if somehow it is more than story and should be taken literally, if not literally it should be picked apart and studied to prove it is not literal and believable anyway.

The early Church theologians and the Celtic Christians read the Bible in a different way. They read it symbolically with imagination. Sometimes they could come up with wild interpretations but if they combined reason with symbolism they often had great incites into the Scriptures. They combined this model with prayer and contemplation of the Scriptures, *lectio divina*. This form of meditation came from the desert Christians. In reading the Scriptures you first found a word or phrase that stood out to you in the reading. Then on a second reading you put yourself into the reading, how did the incident or idea affect you? Finally, what is God teaching you? How should you change or what should you do as a result? *Lectio divina* made Scripture a literal part of the praxis of Christianity.

The theology of this form of interpretation came from Origen, *adimantios,* the "man of steel," so-called because of his asceticism which he took to extremes. Origen was born in Alexandria in 185 C.E. and died in 253 C.E. Origen wrote that the task of exegesis of the Bible was twofold: grasping the grammatical sense of the words and discovering the historical reality of the passage. To deny that a passage was to be taken literally was not merely to say it did not happen historically; also, it was that the grammatical meaning of the words did not contain a deeper message for believers. The interpreter must look for a symbolic meaning of the Scripture within reason and the knowledge of God. This was how Scripture became sacramental. Origen criticized those who did not believe in the Scriptures because they had risen above them spiritually in contemplation:

> If you try to reduce the divine meaning to the purely external significance of the words, the Word will have no reason to come down to you. It will return to its secret dwelling which is contemplation worthy of it. For it has wings, this divine meaning, given to it by the Holy Spirit who is its guide. . . . But to be unwilling ever to rise above the letter, never to give up feeding on the literal sense, is the mark of a life of falsehood.[16]

Are we living "a life of falsehood"? We need to see the symbolic truth in Scripture, not trying to prove everything to be literally true or dismissing it altogether when it is not. The Celtic people interpreted the Bible in this way. It was directed

[16] Clément, *The Roots of Christian Mysticism,* 99.

toward using the Bible in a mystical way rather than a literal way. It was not reading the Bible to believe things about God or Jesus but to believe in the heart. For this reason Celtic people loved the Gospel of John because it is a mystical Gospel not a historical Gospel. It was meant to help people believe Jesus in a mystical way. Often this was the only Gospel carried by Celtic evangelists. Cuthbert, for example, memorized the Gospel of John and a copy was found with his remains when they were exhumed.[17]

The center of Celtic theology was the reading and interpretation of the Bible. The theologians of the day were bibliophiles who looked for and needed more books all the time. It was as if all the efforts of the years when Celtic society committed everything to memory were transferred to the written word. They spent huge amounts of time and money on books, as books like the *Lindisfarne Gospels* and the *Book of Kells* reveal. Monastic communities collected and preserved books. They also served as publishing houses of their day producing books. The first Bible used by Celtic Christians was the Old Latin version called the *Itala*. By the end of the sixth century is was replaced by Jerome's Vulgate.[18]

It was John Cassian that encouraged an interest in the Bible. He wrote, "read the sacred books with the same zeal that you read heathen writers and your thoughts will be pure."[19]

The Celtic Christians read the Bible carefully. In Patrick's *Confession and Letter to Coroticus* alone he makes three hundred and forty citations from forty-six books of the Bible.[20] Finian of Clonard was said to have had three thousand Bible students at one point.[21] Many ecclesiastical scholars had fled the continent to Ireland particularly to escape the Huns, Vandals, and other barbarians ravaging Europe. The interpreters also

---

[17] The little red-leather-covered Gospel book is now in the British Library.

[18] Leslie Hardinge, *The Celtic Church in Britain* (London: S.P.C.K., 1972) 31.

[19] Ibid., 33.

[20] Ibid., 29.

[21] Ibid., 34.

used commentaries by many of the early Church teachers such as Ambrose, Aquila, Augustine, Cassian, Gregory, Hilary, Isidore, Jerome, Origen, and Pelagius.[22] They wrote commentaries on their own. Interpretation was literal but by Origen's system of allegorical interpretation. Each interpreter was on their own with no other guidelines and often they would give several interpretations and let the reader chose which one they preferred. Columba was said to have a system he probably evolved from Theodore of Mopsuestia:

> He divided a division with figure, between books of the law, i.e. he divided a division with allegorizing between books of reading i.e. the Law of each, the Old Law and the New Testament . . . he used to distinguish history with sense, morality and mystical interpretation.[23]

A commentary on the Gospel of Mark from ca. 632 of Cummean urging an adoption of the Roman date for Easter interpreted Scripture in this way:

> When Rebecca first saw Issac, she sprang from the camel whereon she was for humility of spirit. So then, the church has sprung from the camel of pride and the evil deeds whereon she had been when she beheld the bridegroom, i.e. Christ.[24]

As we can see interpretation could get some very creative results. The Celtic interpreters had little knowledge of biblical languages and often any collection of commentaries was scanty. They were mainly interested in reading the Bible for preaching. They wrote glosses above the words in their Bibles with ideas for future sermons, a kind of midrash on texts for preaching.[25] Their purpose was twofold, to convey the intent of the author of the biblical passage and to apply it to the

---

[22] Ibid., 35–36.

[23] Ibid., 39.

[24] Kathleen Hughes, *Early Christian Ireland: Introduction to the Sources* (Cambridge: Cambridge University Press, 1972) 198.

[25] Hardinge, *The Celtic Church in Britain*, 42.

daily lives of the hearers.[26] Preaching was also used as a way of teaching and question-and-answer sermons were common.[27]

Biblical interpretation and preaching was mainly done to communicate the Gospel message to the people. To a symbolic right-brained culture the Bible was translated in that way. It provided a way that people could develop their faith through listening to the reading of the Bible in worship and also in teaching. The Bible provided direction for people in living the Gospel message in all aspects of life.

We need to preach from the Scriptures symbolically when it is appropriate. People need to be able to take something home with them each Sunday that they can use in their life in Christ during the week. They need to have the Bible read and interpreted as sacrament. Reading the Bible in this way makes it acceptable and real. New translations of the commentaries of the early Church theologians make consulting the interpretations of the Fathers easier than ever.[28]

We have gone in the wrong direction in the Church for too long. We don't need to prove the existence of God. We don't need to do the right things or receive the punishment of an angry God. We need to live with God as a mystical presence in our life that guides our actions. We need to live our life as a prayer. People need to know and feel that God is real. Humanity has gone without God for too long.

Poetry has always been sacred to the Celtic people. In this poem written in 1959, the Welsh poet D. Gwenallt Jones expresses the feelings of this chapter.

THE STUMBLING BLOCK

We set the stone against the door of the cave:
  So the pretender could never rise from the grave:
And we spread the news in our writing and talking
  That the body's resurrection was only a myth.

[26] Ibid., 43.
[27] Ibid., 47.
[28] For example, *The Ancient Christian Commentary on Scripture* by Inter Varsity Press, Downers Grove, Illinois.

Our life was governed by the Stalin of reason;
    Reason divorced from the person, understanding
        from the man;
At that time we didn't hear the heart's old reasons
    Or the spirit's voice: man was not two, but one.

When the atom was split, our materialism was split,
    The old marriage of mind and flesh was discovered:
Man was not one, but three—body, soul and spirit;
    The old, poor, restless, needy Trinity.

Flesh quarreling with spirit, spirit arguing with flesh
    Within the narrow circle of self's arrogance:
And in the crisis the Spirit was heard opening the
        Scripture
To sinners traveling on the road to Emmaus.

Our foundations were so unstable; our certainty was so
        rotten;
So shaky in a court, for it was impudently unfair
    To set our evidence against the evidence of those
        who were there,
The testimony of the eleven's eyes and ears.

After our defeat in the court the spirit helped us
    Gradually to move the stone from the grave:
And we smelt Mary's perfumes there, and saw the
        emptiness
    And the cloths and napkin set out so tidy and neat.[29]

---

[29] Donald Allchin, D. Densil Morgan, and Patrick Thomas, *Sensuous Glory: The Poetic Vision of D. Gwenallt Jones* (Norwich: Canterbury Press, 2000) 142; "The Stumbling Block" reprinted by permission of Gomer Press.

Chapter Six

A Crisis of Lifestyle

In 1997 Don Cupitt wrote in his book *After God: The Future of Religion,* that the best thing to do in this time of great change in religion "is to continue to practice one's own local and traditional faith, but on a strictly nonrealistic or consistently demythologized basis." Continue doing what you are practicing in religion but realize that all the symbols are not relevant and they should be viewed with reason. He says members of the Sea of Faith movement believe in a nonrealistic reading of Christianity. They believe:

(1) God is the "religious ideal"—that is, a unifying symbol of our common values and of the goal of our religious life.

(2) The God of Christians is love—that is, the Christian specification of the religious ideal makes agapeic (disinterested, or "solar") love the highest value.

(3) We see love as taking the form of Jesus—in the stories told by and about him, and in the various doctrinal and other stories that have subsequently developed around him.[1]

---

[1] Don Cupitt, *After God: The Future of Religion* (New York: Basis Books, 1997) 127–28.

Cupitt says this minimalist Christian theology derives from Kant and the Ritschlians in Germany. With this theology "one can continue to be a Christian (of sorts) without having to profess any true or irrational beliefs."[2] The only thing to do, after you reject all of the old theistic elements of religion, is to live life fully in love burning out like the sun, "solar ethics." One needs to be an exceptionally good person and live and love fully. This is what we need to do after theism. We cannot wait long for the Church to change to this new way of thinking, Cupitt writes.

Bishop John Spong, in a recent address at St. Deiniol's Library in Hawarden, Wales, on the future of the Church, said basically the same thing.[3] Jesus is the ultimate example of what humanity can become. To just follow Jesus is not enough. He has to be a source of empowerment. We can never be fully human unless we lay down our power, our fears, our defenses. We are not yet complete as human beings and Jesus is our guide to change.

Jesus broke the boundaries of tribal identity of the Jews to include the Gentiles. He walked across the frontiers of prejudice to include Samaritans, lepers, and sinners. He broke the gender barrier and included women such as Mary Magdalene into the inner circle of his apostles. Jesus calls us to cross the final barrier of religion and invites all people of all faiths to live fully. Jesus is God without limits, the Ground of Being. The only thing we can do once we abandon the theistic God is to embrace the example of Jesus, "to live fully, love wastefully, being all we can be."

Two of the most vocal theologians calling for change have developed similar solutions to the challenge to translate the meaning of Christianity into the language of our time so people will understand the Gospel. It is to live as an example of Christ. To live fully and to develop into the person you were created to be was the ultimate spiritual goal of the Celtic Christians. It was the constant destination of the circular spiritual

[2] Ibid.
[3] October 6, 2000.

journey, with no beginning or the end, always a new beginning. It was the "place of resurrection."

The spiritual journey was the concept of spirituality that the Celtic people retained from their culture, but also part of the theology of the desert and the Fathers. It was also in response to a dominant culture that was mostly non-Christian. The hermits and monastics in the desert were reacting to the adaptation of the Church as an accepted, if not dominant part of society. The early Church theologians were developing and teaching a new religion. The early Celtic Christians were relating to a culture that was non-Christian but also very tolerant of diversity and a variety of religious beliefs. Often each geographical area or clan had different local gods and religious practices. To be noticed and recognized as different, the early Celtic Christian lifestyle had to be exceptional.

The same is true in our time in the Western world. As we have read before, a recent survey in the United States asked people if they believed in God. The majority of people said "yes" but they did not attend church. When asked why they did not go to church there were a variety of answers but they can be summarized by the answer "because the church doesn't do anything that makes a difference" and "people who attend church are no different than me." We have a third crisis of our time, the crisis of lifestyle. The crisis simply put is that most people don't believe *us* anymore.

People don't believe we really mean what we say and do, and why should they? We haven't given them what they need, faith and community. We tend to argue over issues that are trivial or unimportant to most people. As mentioned earlier, they are interested more in the "middle things" of life such as getting and keeping a job, going to school, developing relationships, and providing for and living with family and friends. People are concerned mostly with the practical things of life. Faith has to be practical and realistic too. Most of the time the Church appears to be totally out of touch with reality.

Church people get upset about and discuss issues that most people have resolved or do not consider most important in their lives. The morality of homosexuality is not a vital issue. Most people do not stay awake at night worrying that somewhere, somehow other people could be having immoral sex. They are too busy with life to be concerned. They don't care about theology, Kant, Heidegger, or Tillich; they just want to feel the presence of God. There are a few people who still think women should not be ordained. Why are they all in the Church?

We need to show people we believe what we say, otherwise we are no different and we don't make a difference so we are not needed. The Church needs to show evidence of its efficacy and reality. The challenge is to do this in a society where everyone is basically good and law abiding but eager for spiritual growth. The distinctions between the "religious" and "nonreligious" are often blurred.

As we have discussed in chapter 4, the method of Celtic evangelism was "belonging before believing." An essential aspect of this way of bringing people into faith and community is lifestyle. You have to live in a way other people want to emulate. Your way of living must be holy. Evangelism by example may be the best way of all.

The best example of this way of evangelism by lifestyle is the most famous Celtic saint, St. Patrick. We know more about Patrick than many other Celtic saints because two of his own writings still exist, his *Confessions* where he tells us his story and the *Letter to Coroticus* written to a British chief and pirate concerning people stolen from Ireland and forced into slavery. Patrick was born in the late fourth century in northeast Wales. His family was Celtic Roman and Christian. Patrick's grandfather was a priest and his father was a deacon and worked in the Roman government. With many people of his land Patrick was as much Celt as Roman; the two cultures in four hundred years of Roman residence had combined in many ways. Like many young people Patrick rebelled against his upbringing by his wild lifestyle. When he was sixteen he was captured by Irish pirates and sold as a slave in Ireland. Patrick was sold to a prosperous tribal chief and a druid named Miliuc moccu Boin. Miluic put Patrick to work herding sheep.

Patrick's life as a slave sounds much like the story of the Prodigal Son. Patrick had lost everything. He lived out in the open without so much as a coat to keep warm. He had little to eat and literally lived with the cows and sheep he herded. Patrick said that in his distress he began to pray a number of times each day. Eventually he prayed up to a hundred times each day and night. The "love and fear of God" came to Patrick. Like many people of his time, as in ours, Patrick felt that people were punished by God for their sins.[4] He was being punished because he was a slave. Patrick also knew from his upbringing that God would give him strength and grace in his suffering. His crying "Abba Father" brought Patrick to a deep relationship with God in Christ.

After six years of captivity Patrick was told in a dream that a ship was ready to take him home. Patrick walked to the coast where he saw a ship and negotiated his way on board. We know little of what happened in Patrick's life next except that after a shipwreck it took him perhaps years to get home. In some way Patrick became acquainted with the monastic movement and studied to become a priest. He served in ministry when he returned to Wales.

What is most remarkable is that Patrick went back to Ireland. He was finally home and comfortable with his own people and must have been a recognized leader in his community. Patrick began to have dreams at night. An angel named Victor appeared in a dream with letters from his former captors. Patrick then imagined in his dream the people he had known in Ireland, emerging from the forest around his old home. They cried out, "we appeal to you, holy servant boy, to come and walk among us."[5] Patrick appealed to his superiors, was ordained a bishop, and sent on mission to Ireland. The traditional date of his arrival in Ireland with a small entourage is 432 C.E.

Patrick was the first missionary to be appointed by the Church since the apostolic era. The early Church had sent out missionaries with the apostles; for instance, Thomas, who tradition has it traveled and planted churches as far as India. Since the apostles, the Church became content to do ministry

[4] O'Loughlin, *Celtic Theology*, 31.
[5] See Hunter, *The Celtic Way of Evangelism*, 15.

within the Roman Empire. The presumption was that those outside the Roman culture, as we have seen, were barbarians incapable of understanding. Patrick was the first to go out into the "uncivilized" world. The fact that he left his home for Ireland is even more astounding when we understand that the "civilized world" was eroding for Patrick and his contemporaries.

In Patrick's time the whole culture of Rome fell apart. It was a change such as people never imagined in their worst dreams as if the whole structure of society disappeared. It would be the world many of us imagine would emerge after a global nuclear war when everything we know in society and culture was obliterated. Wales was attacked on three fronts. The Anglo-Saxons invaded from the east. The Picts in the north saw a new opportunity for conquest in the south. The Irish pushed by over population and clan wars began to colonize across the Irish Sea in Wales. It was a time of general lawlessness as Patrick's *Letter to Coroticus* reveals; where once the Irish pirates attacked Wales now the Welsh were raiding Ireland for slaves and booty as well. Now Patrick was going to a place the world regarded as literally the end of the earth.[6]

Patrick did not see the Irish as uncivilized; in a way they had become his people. He and the Irish shared a Celtic culture. He knew them and their language and ways. Patrick was willing to leave the organized Church and go to people whom he felt needed God. Patrick did something out of the ordinary paradigm of Church thinking on mission.

We need to do the same thing in our time. If there are many people "in exile" as Bishop Spong contends then we have a ready field for mission. Rather than stay inside Church culture we need to go into popular culture. This is what Patrick did; his genius and that of other Celtic evangelists were taking the Church into the popular dominant culture. They marked the standing stones with the signs of the cross.[7] They told the

---

[6] O'Loughlin, *Celtic Theology*, 37.

[7] An example is St. Samson who during his travels in Cornwall came upon some people dancing around a standing stone. He remonstrated

story of the Gospel in imaginative ways. They preached to the needs of the people. They located their communities in places that were holy in the sacred geography but also they were accessible to people. They built their communities based upon the dun forts and the clan society of the culture. They did mission and ministry within their culture, rather then impose an outside form of Christianity on the people.

The Church of today needs leaders like Patrick who are able to go into the popular culture of today, no matter where they are located, and communicate the Gospel in the way of the people. The best of popular music needs to be used. Modern art needs to be employed to create new symbols for worship. The liturgy needs to be in the language of the people.

There were other missionaries in Ireland when Patrick arrived, mainly in the south of Ireland such as Declan of Ardmore, who had come from Wales years before Patrick. Within less than two hundred years later most of Ireland was Christian. Yet we see in Celtic Christianity many of the elements of pagan Celtic religion. The early Celtic evangelists converted Ireland with no martyrs. There is no substantiated evidence that anyone died in the process of Celtic mission in Ireland. Later on the Roman Christians accused the Celtic missionaries of being too ready to combine Christianity with pagan culture. To Rome no martyrs meant no true faith.

Patrick also was a leader in speaking out against slavery. He wrote to Coroticus condemning him for stealing and enslaving God's children. He was the first person in history to condemn the accepted paradigm of slavery. Patrick knew, after being a slave himself, how incompatible the practice was with the compassion taught by Christ. He was courageous and inspired to speak out in opposition.

The Celtic saints were set aside as people who best exemplified the life of Christ. In some way people saw divinity in

---

the people but instead of destroying the stone he cut a cross on it. The revelers gave up their dancing that year to resume it the next anniversary. S. Baring-Gould and John Fisher, *Lives of the British Saints* (Lampeter, Wales: Llanerch Enterprises, 1990) 107.

what Christ said and did; the God-presence went with Jesus. Celtic saints had the same presence. The hagiographies, the lives of the saints, are not meant to be historical records. They are stories that portray the power and sanctity of the saint. The magical stories of their miracles, their mysterious powers, their oneness with the natural world, and their wisdom, symbolically reveal their sanctity. Most of the lives of the saints were written long after the death of the saint. They were written mainly to show that the community the saint founded was most worthy to be given authority.

In a way the monastic communities were telling the stories of their past rectors and parishioners. A community records the stories of past leaders, events, challenges, successes, and failures. Many Celtic Christian communities did just that in their annals and the life of the local saint. The community, as we have learned, was formed around the life and ministry of the founding saint who now remained with the community even in death at the shrine of the saint within the sacred circle. The people in the Christian community regarded themselves as members of the saint's Christian clan or family.

Besides the spectacular lives of the saints many aspects of the lives of Celtic saints seem very human and not what many people would regard as saintly at all. The Celtic saints are not perfect people who are unbelievably sinless. It's much easier to believe in a saint who was not perfect all the time than one who is clean "as the driven snow." Columcille or Columba is reputed to have left Ireland because he copied a book secretly without permission. In the first recorded copyright dispute he was ordered to return the copy. He refused and caused a battle between the clans involved.[8] Celtic saints also had tempers and cursed people they didn't like regularly. In Patrick's great confrontation with the High King's druids at Tara he lifted a man who challenged him by telepathy and flung him to earth with such force that he died.[9] Life in the community

---

[8] James Charles Roy, *Island of Storm* (Chester Springs, Pennsylvania: Dufour Editions Inc., 1991) 18.

[9] Bamford and Marsh, *Celtic Christianity*, 46.

of Dewi Sant or David of Wales was not absolutely peace-filled either. On one occasion David's steward tried to murder Aidan, his favorite disciple. On another occasion a visiting Irish saint with a fiery temper killed the boy whom David had assigned to wait on him with a single blow of his fist. Even with these lapses from Christian manners, David's rule was harsher than most to the point that some of his monk's didn't like it. David's steward, cook, and his deacon tried to poison him.[10] Often the lives of the saints are filled with tragic violence rather than just stupendous miracles and triumphant events. This is most true in Wales. Wales was the center of the clash between invading people in Britain when the Roman legions left to defend Rome from the barbarians in 410 C.E. Everything was chaos; it was a time of violence, political turmoil and uncertainty, like much of the world today. The saints of Wales as well as St. Patrick lived in this period of cultural upheaval.

The presence of violence and misogyny is most exemplified in the lives of three women saints in Wales. They all fled from suitors they did not want to marry; they were all set on the celibate life of a saint. The first was St. Eluned, "a young woman who from earliest childhood had decided to devote herself to God's service. When a princely suitor appeared who was favored by her parents, Eluned ran away in disguise and tried to find refuge in the nearby villages." She was rejected everywhere and without lodging she laid down to rest in the road. She decided as a result to live her life as a hermit and was permitted to build a cell. "Unfortunately her spurned lover tracked her down and killed her. She was buried in her cell, which was converted into a chapel."[11] Gwenfrewi or Winifred didn't fare much better. When a young noble named Caradog made advances to her she rejected him running off to her uncle St. Beuno's chapel. Before she made it to safety Caradog cut her head off with a swipe of his sword.

---

[10] Baring-Gould and Fischer, *Lives of the British Saints,* 67.

[11] Patrick Thomas, *Candle in the Darkness: Celtic Spirituality from Wales* (Llandysul, Wales: Gomer Press, 1993) 41.

The ground opened where her head landed and a spring gushed forth. Her saintly uncle cursed her murderer so fiercely, he melted. Then he restored Gwenfrewi's head to her body and she made a complete recovery, though she still had a scar on her neck. The well is now the holy well, known as St. Winifred's Well in Flintshire.[12]

A third woman saint who was a victim of violence was St. Non the mother of David or Dewi Sant. The author of one of David's hagiographies describes the assault which led to Dewi's conception. Sanctus, king of Ceredigion, saw Non who was "exceedingly beautiful, a modest virgin." Sanctus was filled with desire and violated her "who, neither before nor after this occasion had any intercourse with any other man, but continued in chastity of mind and body, leading a most faithful life . . ."[13] She became pregnant and, as Eluned, was cast out. She gave birth to Dewi outside in the midst of a violent storm. When David was born the rocks broke open at the place a well burst forth. The spring today is St. Non's well at St. David's. Non raised David by herself at that place until he was ready to be received into a monastic community for his education. Non today might be regarded as the saint of unwed mothers. The similarities between her and the Virgin Mary are obvious. The story of Non is believable and like the lives of many women today and in the past.

Many of the saints gave up worldly power rather than take it. Part of the new life in Christ was to renounce all earthy wealth and privilege, putting trust wholly in Christ. Columba was a prince, and could have been a king.[14] Samson's mother was a princess. Petroc was the son of Glywys, king of Glwysing. He left South Wales "rejecting the vanities and transient allurements of the world; desiring worldly for heavenly things, he began to adhere firmly to God, and he gave up his country, his kindred, and at last all things of this world."[15] The rejec-

---

[12] Ibid., 91.
[13] Ibid., 112.
[14] Bramford and Marsh, *Celtic Christianity*, 27.
[15] Baring-Gould and Fisher, *Lives of the British Saints*, 99.

tion of the opportunities of high birth are common among many Celtic saints. This was the white and green martyrdom of the saints. It showed true devotion to Christ. The saints of the Celtic world were often the brightest and best educated of their time, yet they opted for service to Christ over earthly power and wealth.

The Celtic Christians strived to be examples of godly living. As we have seen there was no violence allowed within the monastic enclosure. People observed a rule. Everyone was included and accepted. The communities were spiritual centers of continual prayer. They were centers of learning offering education to anyone. They served as centers for evangelism and ministry. The intent was to make the community the ideal of what God wants and intends for the world, what Christians call God's kingdom. People were converted by belonging to the community. People were moved by example. The Celtic missionaries loved the people, took time to know them, and showed them by example how to live the Christian way of life. If people are accepted and taken seriously and if our actions show the truth of our commitment then people will believe. People are moved by example; it is the most effective evangelism.

It is often difficult to find a religious leader today that is known as an effective example to people. There are saintly people but few identified by those outside of religion circles. People are very cynical and critical of their leaders. When an inspiring leader does appear a scandal will often follow tarnishing a possible saintly example. People need saints, people they can use as guide to life. The outpouring of grief at the sudden death of Princess Diana may show the need for the example of a truly good person. Saints recognized by the Roman Catholic Church often represent the Christendom paradigm to people more that a holy life. The beatified appear to represent more of the Catholic dogma than sanctity. Religious leaders need to show their commitment more than others.

I am reminded of St. Francis of Assisi who lived a life of complete poverty to show his commitment. His order was formed for ministry to the lowest and most rejected people of the time, the lepers. The Celtic saints lived the same type of example. I am not suggesting we ought to require our religious leaders to give up all property. Most church workers are underpaid and overworked. Everyone who is a Christian must live a life that plainly shows a religious commitment. People can readily see our lack of faith commitment by how little we give, by our consumptive lifestyles, by our hedonistic attitude, our desire for wealth and power, and our irregular worship and prayer. We are *no different* than other people in our society; we are not monastic, people who are set aside; we are not people "called out," the *ekklesia*.

Clergy often set the worst examples for people. When a clergy person is accused or convicted in a scandal it only reinforces the opinion that all Christians are hypocrites and the Church is only for the perfect. Clergy also can show poor examples of leadership by being authoritarian, controlling, or "workaholics." Clergy are often the greatest proponents of Christendom model. They also can be lazy, lacking in enthusiasm, cynical, and uninspiring. Life facing the demands of ministry can make them really question their own belief and effectiveness. Clergy have to willingly be an example of the Christian life of compassion, prayer, and mission and live it.

Lay people can do everything as well as clergy. Laypeople are often treated as children. Some clergy act like laypeople know nothing and can do nothing. By doing everything and controlling everything clergy have taught people to be irresponsible and powerless. The attitude is reinforced by our calling priests "father" or "mother," no matter how well intentioned as a title of respect. Bishops sitting on thrones, special titles or vestments all support clericalism. What is needed in leaders is a balance of effective leadership enabling others to do ministry while providing vision and humility.

The lay people, on the other hand, are more than willing to let the priest or pastor take over and do everything. They act irresponsible or powerless or render the leader powerless by their own need to be in control. Magically, when they enter church, many competent laypeople who serve in demanding jobs during the week become totally dependent, waiting to be served. Clergy need to share ministry and lay people must be part of it. Laypeople can do all or most of what clergy do as well or better. I know of no committed priest or minister who would rather not do the things they were called to do as a spiritual leader—to teach, preach, pray and set a vision of hope for the people—than the other tasks demanding their time.

George Barna and other researchers in congregational development have noticed a lack of leadership in the local congregations as well as at the denominational level. Seminaries are not training people to lead. The people attending seminaries, no matter how well intentioned or committed they may be, are not the personality types or lack the skills and insights needed to be effective in leadership. People with leadership qualities are seduced by the promise of bigger salaries, more power, and a better life in other professions or corporate business. The Church faces a crisis of leadership with the crisis of lifestyle.

If the Church really led people it would do lead by giving up power and authority. The power of God working in the world is through God emptying God's self in kenosis. The great hymn in the letter to the Philippians is a guide:

> Let your bearing towards one another arise out of your life in Christ Jesus. For the divine nature was his from the first; yet he did not think to snatch at equality with God, but made himself nothing, assuming the nature of a slave. Bearing the human likeness, revealed in human shape, he humbled himself, and in obedience accepted even death—death on a cross. Therefore God raised him to the heights and bestowed on him the name above all names, that at the name of Jesus every knee should bow-in heaven, on earth, and in the depths-and every tongue confess, "Jesus Christ is Lord" to the Glory of God the Father (2:5-11) (NRSV).

When we empty ourselves of power and authority that is when God begins to work in us. We first of all come to God in our need and vulnerability asking God to become part of us crying for God. God remains in history the beggar who waits at each person's gate with infinite patience, begging for love. God waits in silence which we sometimes reproach God for, but God's silence is in consideration for us. God is waiting for us to open the gate and let the Spirit inside. God will wait until each person comes to God. As Maximus the Confessor put it:

> God has made himself a beggar by reason of his concern
> for us . . . suffering mystically through his tenderness to
> the end of time according to the measure of each one's
> suffering.

Origen wrote, "Christ . . . freely made himself poor for love of humanity, to make us rich."[16] It is in emptying ourselves of power we receive the greater power of God. Some people ask "how could God sacrifice God's own child; what kind of parent could do such a thing and call it love?" The answer is that God did not do the sacrifice; *God was sacrificed.* The real meaning of the cross is that God in Jesus suffers with us and for us. God never leaves us in our time of suffering and need. When we open the gate to God, God joins our suffering and makes us whole. We are free when we know that the true power to heal, create, and celebrate is in giving ourselves to Christ. A Celtic eucharistic prayer ends with this triumphant hymn:

> I rise up clothed in strength of Christ.
> I shall not be imprisoned, I shall not be harmed;
> I shall not be downtrodden, I shall not be left alone;
> I shall not be tainted, I shall not be overwhelmed.
> I go clothed in Christ's white garments;
> I go freed to weave Christ's patterns;
> I go loved to serve Christ's weak ones;
> I go armed to rout Christ's foes.[17]

It is in the cross of Jesus that we are united with God. It was by the kenosis of Jesus as God with us that brought the power of new life. When we empty ourselves of power we receive the power of God to do great things and to be truly free. Maximus the Confessor put it very well—"Christ's death on the cross is a judgement of judgement."[18]

---

[16] Clément, *The Roots of Christian Mysticism,* 56–57.

[17] The Aidan Trust, *Resources for Ministry in the Celtic Tradition.* Red Hull Christian Centre, Snittelfield, Stratford-upon-Avon, United Kingdom.

[18] Clément, *The Roots of Christian Mysticism,* 49.

The Celtic Christians were fixed on the symbolism of the Cross and its meaning. In the oppression of the poor and weak of their society the cross was a true symbol of freedom in suffering. Saints like Eluned, Winifred, and Non were true examples of power in suffering. The saints who gave up power like Columba were examples of leadership in Christ. In a way the men of society gave up being warriors, protecting the women and children and the elderly and the rights and land of the clan for the greater power of the Cross. St. Pedrog, a warrior who broke his spear on the battlefield at the sight of the carnage there, went with the higher power of peace in Christ. He became a hermit in Cornwall.[19] The Cross is a symbol of power, not defeat. It is a symbol of the uniting of God with humanity in the God-Man, Jesus. My favorite Celtic cross is a very primitive one carved on a small slab of stone inside the ruins of St. Non's chapel at St. David's. It is the site of David's conception, his birth, and his early childhood. The cross is of very early origin, perhaps sixth century.[20] It is primitive, a simple circle quartered with a cross. The shaft of the cross is a little crooked and if you look very closely you can see the trace of the arms and legs of a stickman. It is a sign of the man Jesus who on the cross in his emptying united humanity with God. Another vivid example is an early cross in a human shape at Nevern in Pembrokeshire in Wales.

The Church needs leaders that exemplify Christ more than ever in today's world. People in the contemporary world do not trust or abide by the authority of leaders; authority must be earned. The Celtic church communities were lay led by abbots, abbesses, and those appointed to different tasks. They and the clergy were chosen by the authority they or their family earned. Sometimes the offices were transferred from father to son. All leadership was in the example of the founding saint who lived in their midst. The local community was the center for ministry. Especially today we need to follow their example.

[19] Thomas, Patrick, *Candle in the Darkness,* 47.
[20] Bryce, *Symbolism of the Celtic Cross,* 41.

I believe the role of bishops in the Anglican and Roman Catholic communion should be reexamined and changed. In Celtic Christianity power centered in the communities, not the bishop. Bishops served as teachers, the keeper of theology, the person who was the link between different communities, and evangelists. They often led evangelistic teams; they went to the people and related to them and brought them into God's community by belonging and by teaching. They were not powerful administrators. There were no dioceses or other Roman hierarchical structure. It was in the local communities that ministry was organized and happened. Because of their role there were many bishops.

With the risk of controversy this could be a model for the future. I am not suggesting we give up the episcopate or the authority of bishops but modify their role. As Finney suggested, when you are between paradigms a combination of old and new ways of thinking works best. In the future, however, there will be fewer resources and ministry will center in the local parish community. It is at the grassroots that ministry will occur. Why not center bishops in the local parish where they can serve more in their original capacity in the Celtic model? The diocesan functions could revert back to the responsibility of parish people. For example, the canon to the ordinary could serve as the administrator of a larger parish as well as diocesan duties. The diocesan youth director could serve as a youth leader in a local parish and help other parishes as well. Some of the current administrative duties of bishops could be put in the hands of parish clergy. Clergy would be free to do more of their original spiritual role of being with the people, teaching them, bringing them to faith, protecting them, and providing a vision of what the Church can become. The fulfillment of this model would take some self-emptying on the part of many people, especially bishops.

The Celtic Christians tried to live in a way that was an example to others. The communities were examples, as much as possible, of the Christian ideal of community. The people showed others they really lived what they professed. One of the roles of the community and the clergy was to assist people in growing in faith, living the little things of life, and ministry.

The way people were given assistance in Christian life besides teaching, the sacraments and preaching were by two basic methods: penitence and anamcara or "soul friends."

The first way, penitence, has a bad reputation today especially among Protestants and former Catholics. It is viewed as punishment for sins that have angered a theistic God. If you don't expiate these sins God will punish you or in the end you will face damnation. The standard penance or things you do to wipe out sin seem even more ridiculous such as saying Hail Marys.

The whole idea of penance developed during a major impasse in pastoral care in the early Church. It was expected that after baptism people would not sin again. Some people, like Constantine, held off their baptism until their death bed rather than sin after being washed in the sacrament of new birth. People did sin after baptism. The little sins of normal life were easy enough to forgive but what about the big ones? People guilty of the big sins, such as, murder, apostasy and fornication had to go through a process to get back into the congregation. This put more emphasis on the more serious sins rather than the normal ones. If you did commit a bad sin you had one chance to make up; that was all; if you messed up again you would be dismissed from the congregation. Why not put off your baptism and sow a few wild oats before settling down to the religious life?

The whole idea of penance was to get people to work in the lifelong struggle to be like Christ on the spiritual journey. The Irish practically invented penance. It was a way of dealing with the small sins of life in baptism. The whole idea really came from John Cassian who invented a system of penance to help people in their *theosis* and their turning to God, *metanoia*. His idea is one of the visible links between Eastern monasticism and Celtic monasticism. Cassian proposed a set of penance as if to heal a sickness that kept a person from God.[21] This shifted penitence in specific ways.

[21] O'Loughlin, *Celtic Theology,* 53.

1. It was not punishment but medicine.

2. A new emphasis was put on the individual since sin was a sickness needing diagnosis rather than a crime needing prosecution.

3. It was designed over a range of sins therefore it fit into the ongoing lifelong process.[22]

Penance included a "baptism of tears" which was part of the writing of the early Fathers, particularly Gregory Nazianzen. Gregory stressed that the main ingredient needed for forgiveness for sins after baptism was to be sorry and contrite, to be moved to tears. The feeling bad for sins committed took away the need for public penance. The idea of the "baptism of tears" washing away sin is prevalent in the Irish rules in communities. Columba told his monks to "pray until the tears come."

The old Irish laws were another reason for the adoption of penitentials, guides for penance for sins committed. The Irish law covered every possible type of crime or sin. A price was paid to make a crime right. It was to see damage repaired rather than the punishment of the criminal. The shift in the penitentials for the individual was to have something to do to make the sin right and be guided on the continual spiritual journey.

The penitentials assumed that the person would sin again and again; they would often "miss the mark" which is the definition of sin. St. Finian said penitence was part of pilgrimage rather than an achievement.[23] The intention of the penitentials was to heal people rather than punish them. The person is responsible for doing the therapy to become well. Healing and anointing of the sick is part and parcel to penitence. This was seen most dramatically in the penitentials of Finian and Cummean.[24]

The idea of penitence worked; it was a main part of Celtic Christianity within one hundred years of its introduction. Many people criticize the penitentials such as that of Columbanus for being too harsh. Monks were often beaten as a form

---

[22] Ibid., 54.
[23] Ibid., 56–59.
[24] Ibid., 61.

of penance. Monks were given slaps for different offences.[25] The Culdees in the tenth century took their asceticism to a fanatical form. The same phenomenon happened in the desert monastic movement. People tend to slip into a belief that the body is not spiritual and we must punish it or destroy it to approach God. The early Church Fathers, John Cassian, and the early Celtic saints showed their belief that the body and soul are one in their writing and lives. The first penitentials were for ordinary Christian people, not spiritual athletes. The healing of body and soul go together.

The penitentials gave people a way to work on growing in their faith, a deeper relationship with God in Christ. People need guidance in the spiritual life; they need ways they can experience God. A new form of penance in the Church may be a start. In spiritual direction people are given tasks to strengthen their praxis of prayer and contemplation. Recommendations for all different problems could be given always remembering that sin is not something you must punish or wipe out for an angry theistic God but simply straying off of the path on the way to God.

A second way the Celtic Christians enabled people to live a spiritual life in Christ was by providing mentors. When people came to a monastic community they were put into a small group of people that they worked and lived with in the community. Usually the group was ten or less people led by someone chosen because of their great devotion to God.[26] If the group were students the leader would be the teacher who taught not only information and thoughts but faith as well. Finian of Clonard, for example taught many of the great saints such as Columba, Garan and Brenden in a small group.[27] Cuthbert learned with others from St. Boisil.[28]

[25] O'Loughlin points out in his discussion of the Celtic Eucharist that a monk under Columbanus' rule would be slapped six times for leaving a tooth mark on the chalice! *Celtic Theology,* 136.

[26] Hunter, *The Celtic Way of Evangelism,* 48.

[27] Bramford and Marsh, *Celtic Christianity,* 73.

[28] Michael Mitton, *Restoring the Woven Cord: Strands of Celtic Christianity for the Church Today* (London: Darton, Longman and Todd Ltd., 1995) 23–24.

The wisdom of having small groups is becoming part of congregational development today. Parishes find that small groups help maintain a small community feeling as the congregation grows. Small groups are a way to include newcomers and provide an immediate sense of belonging and fellowship. Small groups are formed on a variety of models but they have directions to divide when they grow too large and to always welcome new people to the group. Some small groups always have a vacant chair included at their meeting as a reminder that a new member is always welcome. Small groups can form around every common denominator that draws people together. They may be strictly Christian learning groups such as Bible studies or confirmation classes. They may be interest groups like quilting, bowling, baseball, or needlework. They can be breakfast or dessert groups that meet strictly for support and friendship. The main thing is to keep the groups small and available to people who want to join. Small groups give everyone a chance and a voice no matter how quiet or shy people may be in personality. Celtic Christians employed the wisdom of small group organization in creating a sense of belonging which would lead to a sense of belief.

Another type of mentor that was prevalent in the Celtic Christian world was the "soul friend" or anamcara. The soul friend was a person that acted as a friend as well as a confessor and spiritual director. They were an equal that you could tell your innermost secrets and feelings to in complete confidence. They accepted you and your failings, promoted and strengthened your talents, and guided you in the spiritual life. They might be a friend or a teacher or someone chosen for their great devotion and saintly behavior. They challenged you as well as supported you. Often they became deep friends. Kevin of Glendalough, for instance had a feeling his anamcara, St. Ciaran was sick unto death and rushed to his side to hold him as he died.[29] People went and talked to their anamcara on a regular basis. To have a soul friend was vital to the spiritual life. St. Bridget on meeting a man whose soul friend had just

[29] Ibid., 98.

died said he should find a new one right away; to not have an anamcara was like having a body without a head.[30]

Soul friends could be a model for mentorship in the future of the Church. The system of anamcaras assumes there is a significant amount of godly people who can act in this capacity. They have to be saintly, trustworthy, and knowledgeable. I am not sure we are ready or able to use the model exactly in our society. Spiritual directors are becoming more common and used by many people. A spiritual director could act as the anamcara and prescribe people penance, things to do, to promote a healthy spiritual life. It was Columba's soul friend that may have suggested he go on mission to Scotland as penance and a new direction in his life after he caused the Battle of the Book over his stolen copy of the Gospels.[31] Spiritual directors could do the same vital task in the Church today. Most clergy are not asked to be spiritual guides and are under utilized in this capacity. The teaching of spiritual direction should be incorporated as part of the seminary curriculum as well as courses in prayer and mystical theology. Spiritual directors should be an integral part of each diocese and easily available to counsel and guide people in the spiritual life. A Church without soul friends is like a body without a head, a Church without a heart.

It is vital that Christians lead a lifestyle that is believable to those outside of the Church. We must be examples of saints, people who believe, live, and do the work of Christ in the world. We must live our lives as if they are a prayer, a sacrament, an outward and visible sign of the presence of God. We must be holy; we must be mystics; we must be saints. We must be aware and see that our lives of prayer and action make all the difference.

The most obvious sign that we are the people of God that the Church has something to offer is to be more effective in mission. A legitimate complaint about the Church is that it doesn't do anything, that it doesn't make a difference. If we

[30] Mitton, *Restoring the Woven Cord*, 45.
[31] Roy, *Islands of Storm*, 19.

become a true community and people can feel the presence of God in their lives and become part of divinity, then people will notice a difference in the lives of people of faith, something they want and need. People will also need to see the proof that the Church makes the world a better place.

Constantly we are told and promised in the Scriptures that we will see a world of total peace and fellowship. The lion will lie down with the lamb; swords will be beaten into plowshares; justice will flow down like a mighty stream. Why doesn't it happen? For centuries people have been placated with the answer that peace and justice will come after death. It is a spiritual thing not a literal promise fulfilled on earth. Such and explanation, if not a lie, is no longer adequate. If we believe that God is in the world and alive in Christ, present in the community, changing our humanity into divinity, working out God's kingdom in what we say and do then the promise has to be fulfilled here and now.

Then why doesn't it happen? Why doesn't God just do it? Come, Lord Jesus! I believe God has given us all the tools to make the kingdom, the world God wants and is waiting for us to do it. Then Christ will come, indeed he will be here.

In his book *The Powers That Be: Theology for a New Millennium,* Walter Wink explores the reason why the Church has been so unsuccessful in bringing change for better.

There is always something that keeps the spirit at bay, a cloud we can never seem to penetrate that holds the Church back from transforming the world. Walter Wink calls this hidden wall the Powers. In the Revelation of St. John the writer addresses the "angel" of each congregation rather than the people there. The angel is the spirit of the Church. As we pointed out each community or congregation has a spirit. It is how people would describe or feel about their community. An angel or spirit can stay in a congregation for long periods of time because it is compatible with people's values. For instance if a congregation has successfully ventured out in mission into its surrounding community and incorporated new people it will have a spirit of openness. If the congregation has been betrayed or abused by a clergy person in the past it will retain the memory of that hurt for years to come.

All institutions have a spirit, even the largest of them. Nations have a spirit. In the book of Daniel, chapter 10, the author speaks to the angels of nations. These angels are the Powers. The Powers are not just people or institutions but the spirituality at the core of institutions. Everything comes from God and is answerable to God so spirit enters into each institution. The early Church called these the "powers and dominions"; they saw a spirit in Rome, its leaders, legions, its crucifixion and called it the Beast or Satan. It is the Powers that block us from changing the world.[32]

It is obvious that the Celtic people believed in the "powers and dominions" as well. They are not demons from the movies but much more subtle. Much of Celtic history, particularly in the last three centuries is very tragic, filled with famine, war, and prejudice. It is not until the past twenty years that fewer people immigrated from Celtic lands than were born there. The hurt is fresh in the spirit of Ireland, Wales and Scotland. The early Celtic Christians prayed to be delivered from all the dark forces that prevailed in their world. An example is the famous caim prayer of St. Patrick his Breastplate when he puts on the armor of God:

> I rise today
> > with the power of God to pilot me,
> > God's strength to sustain me,
> > God's wisdom to guide me,
> > God's eye to look ahead for me,
> > God's ear to hear me,
> > God's word to speak for me,
> > God's hand to protect me,
> > God's way before me,
> > God's shield to defend me,
> > God's host to deliver me:
> > > from snares of devils,
> > > from evil temptations,
> > > from nature's failings,
> > > from all who wish to harm me,

---

[32] Walter Wink, *The Powers That Be: Theology for a New Millennium* (New York: Doubleday, 1998) 3.

> far or near,
> alone or in a crowd.
> Around me I gather all these powers
>   against every cruel and merciless force
>   to attack my body and soul,
>   against the charms of false prophets,
>   the black laws of paganism,
>   the false laws of heretics
>   the deceptions of idolatry,
>   against spells cast by women, smiths and druids,
>   and all unlawful knowledge
>   that harms the body and soul.[33]

To understand what the Powers are we need to understand several world views concerning our relationship with God. If we want to really be the people God created us to be then we need to block the world views that interfere. It is necessary to know what they are; there are five views concerning God that affect our theology:

1. The *Ancient* world view that is reflected in the Bible. Everything on earth has a heavenly counterpart. If war begins on earth there must be a war in heaven as well. This is a symbolic way of saying that every spiritual reality has spiritual consequences.

2. The *Spiritualist* world view beginning in the second century C.E. challenged the worldview of Judaism. Creation is the fall from God. Things of the earth and the flesh are unspiritual if not evil. The Spiritualist world view is demonstrated by Gnosticism, Manichaeism, and Puritanism, and Neoplatonism.

3. The *Materialist* view that there is no heaven, only the material of earth. If you can't see it, hear it or feel it, it doesn't exist. Matter is ultimate. This is the world view of the Enlightenment and science.

4. The *Theological* worldview was created to deal with the Materialist view. It is that there is a higher spirit-

---

[33] Hunter, *The Celtic Way of Evangelism,* 50–51.

ual realm that cannot be felt with the senses. Science tells religion "how"; religion tells science "why." Religion and science are separate.

5. The *Integral* view sees reality as having an inner and outer aspect. It is visualized as a swirl. Heaven and earth are the outer and inner forms of the same reality. The spirit is at the core of everything. The soul permeates the universe. God is in everything, panentheism.[34]

To understand the idea of the Powers we must be in the Integral worldview. The Celtic people were part of the ancient worldview. They tried to placate the gods by worship and sacrifice. They also had an integral view of things. This is the view of early Celtic Christianity. The spirit of God is in the creation and it is good; everything is interconnected; as A. M. Allchin says, "God's presence makes the world." Because the world is God is. "The Powers are good; The Powers are fallen; The Powers must be redeemed," says Wink.[35]

The Powers are part of the integral nature of things; they can be good or evil and fallen at the same time, kind of like people, and they are worthy of being redeemed like people. Christians must believe in this integral view of the world and the Powers to make any difference. As Wink puts it:

> God is at one and the same time upholds a given political or economic system, since some such system is required to support human life; condemns that system insofar as it is destructive of fully human life; and presses for its transformation into a more human order. Conservatives stress the first, revolutionaries the second, reformers the third. The Christian is expected to hold all three.[36]

The integral worldview keeps us from accepting things as they are ("there will always be war" or "the hungry will always be with us") and it keeps us from naming enemies as the

---

[34] Wink, *The Powers That Be,* 15–19.
[35] Ibid., 31.
[36] Ibid., 32.

demons. We are part of the Powers and at the same time we want them to serve humankind not keeping the potential of God from the world.

A few years ago I was priest at a parish in Great Falls, Montana. The main employer of the city is the air force base where most of the nuclear missiles in the United States are deployed. The residents joke that if Montana seceded from the Union the state would be the third nuclear power of the world! The United States Air force has the power at that one site to destroy much of the world once if not many times over. In the 1980s the threat was very real in the midst of the Cold War. The missile base is an example of what the biblical writers called the Powers. It has a good and a bad aspect.

First of all, it supported the city economically. The base provided jobs for civilians and the military spent their pay and lived in the community. The people who worked inside the base on the missiles were just like other people. They were often admired as the protectors of the freedom we all enjoy as Americans. We all pay for the protection of the missiles as part of our taxes. We are part of the system. This was the good aspect of the base. On the fallen side the base held the possibility of unthinkable horrors, the end of life as we know it. There was the visible communist enemy who would overwhelm us if it was not kept at bay. The missiles of both sides were deployed out of fear, armed and ready to fly to kill the enemy like a game of Russian roulette with a pistol in the hand of each side pointed at the head of the other. People in the world still live with this threat and Great Falls was at "ground zero," one of the first places the enemy would hit in the event of the war. Billions of dollars in resources had been spent on the missiles housed in the silos. The dollars were resources taken from the economy that could only be spent for one thing—death—nothing more; the resources were wasted forever. The greatest evil was the missiles would be used to destroy our enemies literally as they killed us, a kind of reciprocal suicide of fear.

This whole system of the powers was supplied by the most prevalent of belief in our society and the world. It is the myth that violence is redemptive. It is the belief that killing the enemy or the villain brings peace and redeems, makes things right. We see this myth in movies and stories where the hero is hurt by the villain but then conquers in the end. We see it in everything from the cartoon Popeye to the violent movie *Gladiator*. It is the myth that is taught to our children, particularly boys, over and over again. Walter Wink writes that "the myth of redemptive violence is the simplest, laziest, most exciting, uncomplicated, irrational and primitive depiction of evil the world has ever known."[37]

This myth keeps everything like normal and the powerful in control of the Powers that keep the world from being the place God intended. It helps people think that evil is outside of ourselves, someone different is at fault, a person from a different country or way of thinking, of a different color or sexual orientation, or even the opposite sex. When the system of the Powers is challenged it can react with unbelievable violence.

When I lived in Great Falls I always felt the ladies in my midweek Bible study could bring the system of the Powers in our community to its knees. They were saints. They were just like the women who meet in every church meeting in the daytime Monday through Friday. They were not young usually, but wise. They were not fanatics or the overly religious or opinionated. They weren't hippies or radicals. They were people of prayer. They were respected and protected in the community.

It was a crime to enter the missile base without permission. Each year a whole group of demonstrators did just that and were arrested by the military police, many of whom thought the demonstrators were part of a communist plot or just plain nuts. The ladies in my Bible study could walk into the missile base and what could they do?

The role of the Church, the *ekklesia,* is to call these Powers back to their divine vocation, their good calling. The wisdom of God in its rich variety is made known to the rulers and authorities of the world (Eph 3:10).[38] No institution is worthy of existence if it does not benefit the people. It is the community's job to bring the divine purpose back to institutions,

---

[37] Ibid., 53.
[38] Ibid., 29.

organized communities whether they be city government, a local club, or the nations.

The Church does this challenging of the Powers by becoming free of the Powers by dying to their control. It is by kenosis the emptying of power and control. It is to be willing to die rather than submit to the command of the Powers. This is what Jesus witnessed to in everything he did in life and in his death. It is what he meant when he said, "he who loses his life will keep it" (Luke 17:33). This is the power of Christianity. It was lost when Christianity became part of the Roman government and the Empire took over the role of providential agent in the world.[39] The way the Church can change the world is to simply be the Church, God's community.

It must be the community of faith in relationship with God in Christ. It must be a community of prayer that teaches prayer and prays without ceasing. It must be a community of outreach. It must challenge any system that has lost its calling to do good.

The Church can change the world; it is the place where transfiguration happens. The early Celtic Christians, I believe, functioned as the Church, God's community, until it too was caught in the web of the Powers in the Roman state. It transformed the Celtic world into a church community for God, the Caim Community. A poem by Waldo Williams, a great Welsh poet of the twentieth century, tells us of the truth and power of the Gospel in Christ:

WHAT IS MAN?

To live, what is it? It's having
A great hall between cramped walls.
To know another, what's that? Having
The same root under the branches.

To believe, what is it? Guarding a town
Until acceptance comes.
Forgiveness, what's that? A way through thorns
To an old enemy's side.

---

[39] Ibid., 89–90.

Singing, what is it? The ancient
Genius of the creation.
What's work but making a song
Of the trees and wheat?

To rule a kingdom, what's that? A craft
That is crawling still.
And to arm it? You put a knife
In a baby's hand.

Being a nation, what is it? A gift
In the depths of the heart.
Patriotism, what's that? Keeping house
In a cloud of witnesses.

What's the world to the strong?
Hoop a-rolling.
To the children of the earth, what is it?
A cradle rocking.[40]

---

[40] Waldo Williams, *The Peacemakers,* trans. Tony Conran (Landysul, Wales: Gomer Press, 1997) 131; "What is Man?" reprinted with permission of Gomer Press.

Conclusion

Some people ask why we should work to save the Church. If the institution cannot change fast enough to relate to people in our time maybe we should let it die. The Church can take long periods of time to change and see things in a new light. Maybe the Church has to die before it can be born again. Certainly the Church will never die because it is the Body of Christ. If it dies in its current incarnation it will be reborn in the Spirit doing things in a new way no one can even imagine.

Arlin Rothauge has found in his research that the life cycle of congregations is like the cycle of life. Each person and each created being goes through a life cycle from birth to death. Life is a great circle as the Celts envisioned with all of us joining with our Creator at the end, the place where we began. The Church year and the faith journey are lived out in the same way. Birth is celebrated in Advent and Christmas. Formation in life and growing up is observed in the season of Epiphany. The stability of life when goals are accomplished is lived in Pentecost. The decline of life is experienced in the season of Lent. Then, the cycle begins all over again in rebirth at Easter. Rothauge asserts that the same life cycle is lived in parish churches. Congregations go from life to death.[1] Congregational

---

[1] Arlin Rothauge, *The Life Cycle in Congregations: A Process of Natural Creation and an Opportunity for New Creation* (New York: Congregational Development Services, Episcopal Church Center) 3–14.

development is enabling them to experience new birth by beginning new life before a decline begins in the period of stability. He calls the beginning of new things while the old continues "parallel development."[2] This is the "two tiered" model of the Celtic Christians in ministry.

Our congregations and the Church can be given new life in the same way. While it is true that many congregations are perhaps too far in the process to be revived many of our congregations can begin a new life if they are willing to change and embrace a new paradigm for ministry. I believe that when congregations thrive as true communities they are renewed by the Spirit of God in *perichoresis*. The cycle of new life is lived over and over again. Our congregations do not have to die; renewal of the congregation is an eternal process in God.

Jesus was transfigured on the mountain with his disciples (Matthew 17:1-9). He had gone up on the mountain to pray and to discern what he should continue to do in his ministry. Likewise we are faced with a decision of what we must do to meet the challenge of the crises we face. We need to be changed into a new type of Church, transfigured to the Church God wants us to be. To be transfigured is nothing less than the goal and purpose of the Church. The Church is a place of new birth; it is a place to be reborn in all the aspects of life.

Jesus was transfigured on the mountain and made a new person by God. "In their presence he was transfigured; his face shone like the sun, and his clothes became white as light." Because Jesus represents all humanity and we are part of him we can be transfigured and changed to live in God's way too. The Church is the sacramental presence of Jesus, the Risen One, who has shown us we are given new life. The Church might be called the Pneumatosphere in which the Spirit of God exists to make the transfiguration of us but also of all creation. Olivier Clement writes, "The Spirit abounds most plentifully in the sacramental body of Christ, but wherever

[2] Arlin Rothauge, *Parallel Development: A Pathway for Exploring Change and a New Future in Congregational Life* (New York: Congregational Development Services, Episcopal Church Center) 12.

the Spirit is at work in history and in the universe, the Church is secretly present. There is not a blade of grass that does not grow within the Church, not a constellation that does not gravitate towards her, every quest for truth, for justice, for beauty is made within her, every scrape of meditation, of wisdom, of celebration is gathered in by her" and transfigured into God in the world.[3]

The Spirit of God is in community; community is the Church. To let our churches die is to deny our true purpose and sacrifice the communities, the places God has given us to grow into Divinity. If the churches die how nonspiritual could the world get? Many people have simply forgotten how to be spiritual. Do we have the time to waste? We must use the resources we have now to begin to be the Church and Transfigure the Universe.

The Spirit of God works in the community of the Church to transform us. We, first of all, cry out to God and ask for God's help (grace) in our lives. There is a turning to God *(metanoia)* and in the turning to God, God embraces us and takes us into the Divine. Then we empty ourselves *(kenosis)* and give ourselves to God. It is in constant turning and giving that we are deified, made part of God *(theosis)*. In the community the Spirit is intensified and there is an energy that creates more energy for transformation *(perichoresis)*. We are transfigured in Christ into his Body and the Creation with us.

All of us personally and as a Church need to make the commitment to *metanoia,* a turning to Christ and begin the process of deification. We need to pray in the words of an eighth-century Celtic monk:

> Dear, chaste Christ,
> Who can see into every heart and read every mind,
> Take hold of my thoughts.
> Bring my thoughts back to me
> And clasp me to yourself.

---

[3] Oliver Clément, *The Roots of Christian Mysticism* (Hyde Park, New York: The New City Press, 1995) 96.

Or this traditional Celtic prayer:

> O Son of God, change my heart.
> Your spirit composes the songs of the birds and the
> buzz of the bees.
> I ask of you only one more miracle:
> Beautify my soul.[4]

The Church and the people in it can be transfigured by the grace of God to be the community God created us to be. We can make the transformation into God's Church with the form of doing mission and ministry modeled by the early Celtic Christians. It is a model that turns our present form of ministry inside out. What do we need to do to make the change?

1. Be a community. Each congregation should strive to be a true community that is inclusive, contemplative, healing and converting, and has the Spirit. They should keep these aspects of community ever before them and evaluate constantly how well they are doing. When they fail in the task the community heals itself and begins anew. All decisions and ministry is based on achieving the elusive vocation of community in the Church.

2. The church should be active in welcoming and inviting people into the community. No one should be excluded and each church should have a newcomer committee to help new members feel they belong. Belonging comes before believing. The goal of the church community is to be a "thin spot" a place where heaven and earth meet and the fulfillment of what God wants becomes reality.

Help people grow in faith. People need to believe in the presence of Christ in the heart, not believing things about Jesus. The church should teach people how to pray, not just with words but in contemplation. There needs to be regular classes in techniques of meditation as well as contemplative prayer. Congregations should have spiritual directors who work with the people. Seminaries need to teach future clergy people prayer but also mystical theology. People need times in community but also solitary experiences to be whole. The local congre-

---

[4] Pat Robson, *A Celtic Liturgy* (London: Harper Collins, 2000) 3.

gation needs to be a place of unceasing prayer. The goal is to live life as if it is a prayer. Mystics, those people who acutely feel the presence of God, need to be accepted and encouraged until everyone feels their true mystical calling. The concept of life as a pilgrimage should be taught and lived by the people.

Members should be encouraged, when they are ready, to make the commitment to live a rule of life. The rule should be used as a guide for becoming a person of prayer, growth in God, and action. It should be attainable and realistic, but challenging. Living a rule helps people to be identified as believers because of their behavior, especially compassion for others. Christian people need to be obviously different than the culture. Their task is to call the culture to its true task, service to God.

Programs for mentors and soul friends should be developed. Small groups can help people feel they belong as well as serve to promote spiritual formation. The church needs to be a center for outreach to the community. A two-tiered approach to ministry needs to be taken. The church should develop a special ministry of evangelism and gather people called to evangelism into teams.

3. Local congregations will be the center of ministry in the future. The Church should reevaluate the role of bishops and administration and the way they serve. Bishops should be relieved of administrative duties and serve primarily as theologians, teachers, evangelists, and the bridge person between congregations. Clergy need to lead by giving up power and control and promoting the ministry of the laity. The local church will be the greatest vehicle for change in the future. With God's help the people of God's community the church can break the dominance system and make the earth the place God intended it to be. The local church is here to stay! It is where God is present in the hearts of the people.

A poem by R. S. Thomas speaks of the promise for the future of the Church:

THE MOON IN LLEYN

The last quarter of the moon
of Jesus gives way
to the dark; the serpent

digests the egg. Here
on my knees in this stone
church, that is full only
of the silent congregation
of shadows and the sea's
sound, it is easy to believe
Yeats was right. Just as though
choirs had not sung, shells
have swallowed them; the tide laps
at the Bible; the bell fetches
no people to the brittle miracle
of the bread. The sand is waiting
for the running back of the grains
in the wall into its blond
glass. Religion is over, and
what will emerge from the body
of the new moon, no one
can say.
    But a voice sounds
in my ear: Why so fast,
mortal? These very seas
are baptized. The parish
has a saint's name time cannot
unfrock. In cities that
have outgrown their promise people
are becoming pilgrims
again, if not to this place,
then to the recreation of it
in their own spirits. You must remain
kneeling. Even as this moon
making its way through the earth's
cumbersome shadow, prayer, too,
has its phases.[5]

---

[5] R. S. Thomas, *Poems of R. S. Thomas* (Fayetteville, Ark.: The University of Arkansas Press, 1985) 96. "The Moon in Lleyn" reprinted by permission of the University of Arkansas Press. Copyright 1975 by R. S. Thomas.

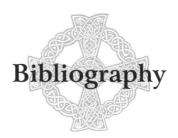

Bibliography

Adam, David. *The Cry of the Deer: Meditations on the Hymn of Patrick*. Wilton, Connecticut: Morehouse-Barlow, 1987.

Adam, James R. *So You Can't Stand Evangelism?: A Thinking Person's Guide to Church Growth*. Cambridge and Boston: Cowley Publications, 1997.

Allchin, A. M., and Esther de Waal, ed. *Daily Readings from Prayers and Praises in the Celtic Tradition*. Springfield, Illinois: Templegate Publishers, 1986.

Allchin, A. M. *The World Is a Wedding*. New York: Oxford University Press, 1978.

Allchin, Donald, D. Densil Morgan, and Patrick Thomas. *Sensuous Glory: The Poetic Vision of D. Gweallt Jones*. Norwich: Canterbury Press, 2000.

Bamford, Christopher, and William Parker Marsh. *Celtic Christianity: Ecology and Holiness*. Great Barrington, Massachusetts: The Lindisfarne Press, 1987.

Baring-Gould, S., and John Fosler, eds. *Lives of the British Saints*. Lampeter, Wales: Llanerch Enterprises, 1990.

Bellah, Robert N. et al. *Habits of the Heart: Individualism and Commitment in American Life*. Berkeley: University of California Press, 1985.

Bitel, Lisa M. *Isle of the Saints: Monastic Settlement and Christian Community in Early Ireland*. Ithaca, New York: Cornell University Press, 1990.

The Book of Escomb: Prayers in the Escomb Tradition. London: Nicolas Deddow.

Booty, John. *The Episcopal Church in Crisis*. Cambridge, Massachusetts: Cowley Publications, 1988.

Borg, Marcus. *Meeting Jesus Again for the First Time: The Historical Jesus and the Heart of Contemporary Faith*. San Francisco: Harper Collins, 1995.

Bosch, David J. *Transforming Mission: Paradigm Shifts in Theology of Mission*. Maryknoll, New York: Orbis Books, 1991.

Bradley, Ian. *Colonies of Heaven: Celtic Models for Today's Church*. London: Darton, Longman and Todd Ltd., 2000.

_____. *The Celtic Way*. London: Darton, Longman, and Todd Ltd., 1993.

Bryce, Derek. *Symbolism of the Celtic Cross*. York Beach, Maine: Samuel Weiser, Inc., 1995.

Cahill, Thomas. *How the Irish Saved Civilization: The Untold Story of Ireland's Heroic Role from the Fall of Rome to the Rise of Medieval Europe*. New York: Doubleday, 1995.

Carmichael, Alexander. *Carmina Gadelica*. Hudson, New York: Lindisfarne Press, 1992.

Clemént, Oliver. *The Roots of Christian Mysticism*. Hyde Park, New York: The New City Press, 1995.

Cupitt, Don. *Solar Ethics*. London: SCM Press, 1995.

_____. *After God: The Future of Religion*. New York: Basis Books, 1997.

_____. *Mysticism After Modernity*. Oxford: Blackwell Publishers, Ltd., 1998.

Davies, Oliver. *Celtic Christianity in Early Medieval Wales: The Origins of the Welsh Spiritual Tradition*. Cardiff: University of Wales Press, 1996.

Davies, Oliver, and Fiona Bowie. *Celtic Christian Spirituality: An Anthology of Medieval and Modern Sources*. New York: Continuum Publishing Company, 1995.

Dean, Eric. *Saint Benedict for the Laity*. Collegeville, Minnesota: The Liturgical Press, 1989.

De Waal, Esther. *A World Made Whole: Rediscovering the Celtic Tradition*. London: Harper Collins, 1991.

_____. *The Celtic Way of Prayer: The Recovery of the Religious Imagination*. London: Hodder and Stoughton, 1996.

De Waal, Esther, ed. *The Celtic Vision: Prayers and Blessings from the Outer Hebrides, Selections from the Carmina Gadelica*. London: Darton, Longman and Todd Ltd., 1995.

Doble, G. H. *Lives of the Welsh Saints*. Cardiff: University of Wales Press, 1971.

Finlay, Ian. *Columba*. London: Victor Gollancz Ltd., 1979.

Finney, John. *Recovering the Past: Celtic and Roman Mission*. London: Darton, Longman and Todd, 1966.

Hanson, Paul D. *The People Called: The Growth of Community in the Bible*. San Francisco: Harper and Row, 1986.

Hardinge, Leslie. *The Celtic Church in Britain*. London: S.P.C.K., 1972.

Harvey, Andrew. *Son of Man: The Mystical Path to Christ*. New York: Jeremy P. Tarcher and Putnam, 1999.

Heaney, Seamus. *Seeing Things*. New York: The Noonday Press, 1991.

Herm, Gerhard. *The Celts*. New York: St. Martin's Press, 1976.

Hughes, Kathleen. *The Church in Early Irish Society*. London: Methuen and Co. Ltd., 1966.

_____. *Early Christian Ireland: Introduction to Sources*. Cambridge: Cambridge University Press, 1972.

Hughes, Kathleen and Ann Hamlin. *Celtic Monasticism: The Modern Traveler to the Early Irish Church*. New York: The Seabury Press, 1977.

Hunter, George G. *Church for the Unchurched*. Nashville: Abingdon Press, 1996.

_____. *The Celtic Way of Evangelism: How Christianity Can Reach the West . . . Again*. Nashville: Abingdon Press, 2000.

James, Simon. *The World of the Celts*. London: Thames and Hudson, 1993.

Lawrence, C. H. *Medieval Monasticism: Forms of Religious Life in Western Europe in the Middle Ages*. London: Longman, 1984.

Life of St. Columba: Adomnan of Iona. Trans. Richard Sharpe. London: Penguin Books, 1995.

Livingstone, E. A., ed. *The Concise Oxford Dictionary of the Christian Church*. Oxford: Oxford University Press, 1977.

Loosky, Vladimir. *The Mystical Theology of the Eastern Church*. London: James Clark and Company Ltd., 1957.

Marsden, John. *Sea Road of the Saints: Celtic Holy Men in the Hebrides*. Edinburgh: Floris Books, 1995.

Mead, Loren. *The Once and Future Church: Reinventing the Congregation for a New Mission Frontier*. New York: The Alban Institute, 1991.

_____. *More Than Numbers: The Ways Churches Grow*. New York: The Alban Institute, 1993.

_____. *Transforming Congregations for the Future*. Washington, D.C.: The Alban Institute, 1994.

Meeks, Wayne H. *The First Urban Christians: The Social World of the Apostle Paul*. New Haven and London: Yale University Press, 1983.

Meyendorff, John. *St. Gregory Palomas and Orthodox Spirituality*. St. Vladimir's Seminary Press, 1974.

Mitton, Michael. *Restoring the Woven Cord: Strands of Celtic Christianity for the Church Today*. London: Darton, Longman and Todd Ltd., 1995.

Mould, Daphne D. C. Pochin. *The Celtic Saints*. New York: MacMillan, 1956.

Mytum, Harold. *The Origins of Early Christian Ireland*. London and New York: Routledge Publishing, 1992.

O'Loughin, Thomas. *Celtic Theology: Humanity, World and God in Early Celtic Writings*. London: Continuum, 2000.

Peck, M. Scott. *The Different Drum: Community Making and Peace*. New York: Simon and Schuster, 1987.

Pelican, Jaroslav. *Maxmimus the Confessor: Selected Writings*. (Introduction). Trans. George G. Borthold. London: S.P.C.K., 1985.

Pennick, Nigel. *Celtic Sacred Landscapes*. New York: Thames and Hudson, 1996.

Rasmussen, Larry L. *Moral Fragments and Moral Community*. Minneapolis: Fortress Press, 1993.

Rhigyfarch. *Life of St. David*. Trans. J. W. James. Cardiff: University of Wales Press, 1967.

Robson, Pat. *A Celtic Liturgy*. London: Harper Collins, 2000.

Roehlkepartain, Eugene C., and Dorothy L. Williams. *Exploring Faith Maturity: A Self Study Guide or Adults*. Minneapolis: Search Institute, 1990.

Roy, James Charles. *The Road Wet, the Wind Close: Celtic Ireland*. Chester Springs, Pennsylvania: Dufour Editions, 1986.

_____. *Islands of Storm*. Chester Springs, Pennsylvania: Dufour Editions, 1991.

St. Benedict. *St. Benedict's Rule for Monasteries*. Trans. Leonard J. Doyle. Collegeville, Minnesota, 1948.

St. Patrick. *The Confession of St. Patrick*. Trans. D. R. Howlett. Ligouri, Missouri: Triumph Books, 1994.

Sample, Tex. *U.S. Lifestyles and Mainline Churches: A Key to Reaching People in the 90's*. Louisville, Ky.: Westminster/ John Knox Press, 1990.

Sellner, Edward C. *Wisdom of the Celtic Saints*. Notre Dame, Indiana: Ave Maria Press, 1993.

Sharkey, John. *Celtic High Crosses of Wales*. Llanrwst, Wales: Gwasg Carreg Gwalch, 1998.

Sheldrake, Phillip. *Living Between Worlds: Place and Journey in Celtic Spirituality*. Cambridge: Cowley Publications, 1995.

Spong, John Shelby. *Why Christianity Must Change or Die: A Bishop Speaks to Believers in Exile: A New Reformation of the Church's Faith and Practice*. San Francisco: Harper Collins, 1998.

Streit, Jakob. *Sun and Cross: From Megalithic Culture to Early Christianity in Ireland*. Edinburgh: Floris Books, 1977.

Thomas, Charles. *Christianity in Roman Britain to A.D. 500*. London: B. T. Batsford Ltd., 1981.

Thomas, Patrick. *Candle in the Darkness: Celtic Spirituality from Wales*. Dyfed, Wales: Gomer Press, 1993.

Thomas, R. S. *Poems of R. S. Thomas*. Fayetteville, Arkansas: The University of Arkansas Press, 1985.

Urban, Linwood. *A Short History of Christian Thought*. Oxford: Oxford University Press, 1995.

Wilken, Robert L. *The Christians As the Romans Saw Them*. New Haven: Yale University Press, 1984.

Williams, Waldo. *The Peacemakers*. Trans. Tony Conran Long. Landysul, Wales: Gomer Press, 1997.

Wilson, A. N. *God's Funeral*. London: John Murray, 1999.

Wink, Walter. *The Powers That Be: Theology for a New Millennium*. New York: Doubleday, 1998.

Wuthnow, Robert. *The Restructuring of American Religion*. Princeton, New Jersey: Princeton University Press, 1988.

Index